Love

is

Love

is

*Loving Others
God's Way*

Laura Martin

CF4·K

10 9 8 7 6 5 4 3 2 1
© Copyright 2012 Laura Martin
ISBN: 978-1-84550-971-2
Published in 2012
by Christian Focus Publications,
Geanies House, Fearn, Tain,
Ross-shire, IV20 1TW,
Great Britain

Cover design by
Daniel van Straaten
Printed and bound by Bell and Bain, Glasgow

FOR MY GIRLS
Georgia, Lucy and Kate.
You are my joy and delight.
I am so thankful to be, and am ever yours,
Mama x

AND FOR MY NIECES
Tegan, Clara, Sophie, Maria, Anna, Tinkerbell,
Myfanwy, Jessica and Jazz.
I love you all very much.
May you grow in the grace and knowledge of
Him who created you.

xx

Contents

1 Corinthians 13

I f I speak in the tongues of men and of angels, but have not love, I am only a resounding gong or a clanging cymbal. [2]If I have the gift of prophecy and can fathom all mysteries and all knowledge, and if I have a faith that can move mountains, but have not love, I am nothing. [3]If I give all I possess to the poor and surrender my body to the flames, but have not love, I gain nothing.

[4]Love is patient, love is kind. It does not envy, it does not boast, it is not proud. [5]It is not rude, it is not self-seeking, it is not easily angered, it keeps no record of wrongs. [6]Love does not delight in evil but rejoices with the truth. [7]It always protects, always trusts, always hopes, always perseveres.

[8]Love never fails. But where there are prophecies, they will cease; where there are tongues, they will be stilled; where there is knowledge, it will pass away. [9]For we know in part and we prophesy in part, [10]but when perfection comes, the imperfect disappears. [11]When I was a child, I talked like a child, I thought like a child, I reasoned like a child. When I

8

became a man, I put childish ways behind me. [12]Now we see but a poor reflection as in a mirror; then we shall see face to face. Now I know in part; then I shall know fully, even as I am fully known.

[13]And now these three remain: faith, hope and love. But the greatest of these is love.

Love is Patient

GOD'S WORD: 1 CORINTHIANS 13:4-8A

When was the last time you had to wait patiently? Maybe it was yesterday when you were waiting in line, or maybe you had to wait for your turn to talk on the telephone. There are lots of times each day when we all need to wait patiently, but sometimes being patient is hard!

The Bible tells us that 'love is patient'? What do you think that means?

Let's think about it. Read this next sentence out loud. Ice is cold. What is the sentence about? Well it's describing ice. But is that all that we say to describe ice? No. What are some other words we use to describe ice?

How about: slippery, wet, frozen water, transparent, dangerous, useful. All of these words and probably lots more that you can think of give us a bigger picture of what ice is like. It's the same with love. Love is not just a nice feeling that we have for our family and friends. There are lots of words which we can use to describe what love is. One of these words is 'patient'. That means if we love someone, we will be patient with them.

As we have already said, sometimes it's not easy to be patient, but we have a wonderful example of someone we can follow who is the most patient person ever! Who? Jesus!

Let's Read
Turn in your Bible to Luke 9:46-48

An argument started among the disciples as to which of them would be the greatest. Jesus, knowing their thoughts, took a little child and had him stand beside Him. Then He said to them, 'Whoever welcomes this little child in my name welcomes me; and whoever welcomes me welcomes the one who sent me. For he who is least among you all – he is the greatest.'

The disciples were arguing over who of them was the greatest or the best. They should have known that Jesus wasn't looking for someone to be the greatest or the best – He just wanted them to love Him and obey Him by loving others. Even so, instead of being cross over

12

their silly argument He was patient with them and explained to them what being the greatest really meant.

Digging Deeper

* When the disciples were arguing about being the greatest, was that showing love to one another? How could they have shown love to one another instead of arguing?

* Why is it so hard sometimes to be patient with someone? When do you find it especially hard to be patient with someone? What can you do or what attitude can you have to overcome this?

* What did Jesus mean when He said, 'For he who is least among you all – he is the greatest'?

* What is the opposite of 'patience'? What other attitudes do you think we might show when we are impatient? What do we need to do about these attitudes?

* What three things would you like the Lord to help you be more patient with? It might be waiting in line for your turn, or patience when a younger brother or sister is learning to play a game with you. Or maybe it's patience when your mum or

13

dad isn't able to help straight away. The Lord wants us to show love to those around us by being patient. He would love to help you.

- Once you have thought about these three things, add them to the prayer written below.

Let's Pray

*D*ear Lord, thank you for the example that you are to us of being patient. Please forgive me for the times when I am impatient. Please help me to be patient – especially in these three areas:

1. brothers and sisters
2. playing games
3. when you want to leave

Please help people to see my love for them in the way that I am patient with them. And please help me to remember just how patient you are with me.

In your name, Jesus,
Amen

The Good Shepherd

GOD'S WORD: PSALM 23

Are you familiar with what a shepherd does? Have you watched one in action or seen one in the distance on a mountainside or far-off field?

Psalm 23 is a well-known passage of scripture that shows us how much care a shepherd takes over his sheep and how much care God takes over us.

Let's Read
Turn in your Bible to Psalm 23

The LORD is my shepherd I shall not be in want. He makes me lie down in green pastures, He leads me beside quiet waters, He restores my soul.

He guides me in paths of righteousness for His name's sake. Even though I walk through the valley of the shadow of death, I will fear no evil, for you are with me; your rod and your staff, they comfort me. You prepare a table before me in the presence of my enemies. You anoint my head with oil; my cup overflows.

Surely goodness and love will follow me all the days of my life, and I will dwell in the house of the LORD forever.

Psalm 23 was written by a shepherd-boy called David. He knew all about caring for sheep because when he was younger, that was his job. In order to care for the sheep he had to know all about the dangers they would face – the wild animals, the thieves, the lack of water and food.

David's job as shepherd was not only to protect his sheep, but also to provide for them.

David was also a songwriter and he wrote songs of worship to God. Psalm 23 is one of those songs. When David wrote about God as a Shepherd, he knew how much a shepherd loves his sheep – and he saw that this was a beautiful picture of how God loves his people – by providing for them and protecting them.

Digging Deeper

- Who is 'my shepherd'? (v.1)
- What is the job of a shepherd?
- What are four things from Psalm 23 that the Lord our Shepherd does for His people?

  1.
  2.
  3.
  4.

- The answers that you have written are wonderful examples of ways that the Lord shows His love for His people. What are some other ways that the Lord shows His love for His people?
- How do we become one of the Lord's children?
- What does verse 6 mean for Christians?
- When we pray to the Lord, our Shepherd, we can pray the words that are written in the Bible. We can pray about the things He has promised us. We can ask for forgiveness for our sins.
- Today when we pray, we will thank God for some of the things that He does for His people and we will use the answers that you have written for question three.

Let's Pray

Dear God, thank you that you are the Shepherd of your people and that you show your love for your people by the way that you care for them and look after them. David knew exactly what it was to be a shepherd and he saw that you show that same love to your people. As we read Psalm 23 I want to thank you for these ways that you show your love to your people.

1. You.....
2. You....
3. You...
4. You...

Please help me also to show love to people by the way I care for them.

In Jesus' name,

Amen

Love is Kind

GOD'S WORD: 1 CORINTHIANS 13:4-8A

About 150 years ago there was a doctor called David Livingstone. He went to Africa as a missionary to tell people about the Lord Jesus.

David Livingstone did many wonderful things in Africa. One story tells us of how his kindness towards a little girl showed her people how he loved them.

One day David Livingstone went to a village where white men had not been before. The people of the village were known to be angry and hard-hearted, but David Livingstone knew that they needed to hear about Jesus, just like everyone else.

When he went to the village he found the chief's young daughter was very sick. The African witch doctor had not been able to heal the girl and so her father told David Livingstone that he must heal the girl – but if the girl died, he would lose his life too.

What a frightening thing that must have been for David. But he knew that Jesus loved the chief and all the people in the village, so he agreed to try and help the sick girl. The Lord helped David and the girl was made well. Imagine the rejoicing of the chief and his wife over the healing of their daughter. Then David was able to tell the people about his great God – the God who saves people from their sin.

David Livingstone showed the chief and his family a great kindness. Even though it must have been frightening for him, he chose to stay and help the girl because he knew that by loving the African people and showing them kindness they would want to listen to what he had to tell them about Jesus. Even more wonderful is that the African chief believed in Jesus and was saved.

Let's Read
Turn in your Bible to Matthew 9:1-8

Jesus stepped into a boat, crossed over and came to His own town. Some men brought to Him a paralytic, lying on a mat. When Jesus saw their faith, He said to the paralytic, 'Take heart, son; your sins are forgiven.' At this, some of the teachers of the law said to themselves, 'This fellow is blaspheming!'

20

Knowing their thoughts, Jesus said, 'Why do you entertain evil thoughts in your hearts? Which is easier: to say, "Your sins are forgiven," or to say, "Get up and walk"? But so that you may know that the Son of Man has authority on earth to forgive sins...' Then He said to the paralytic, 'Get up, take your mat and go home.' And the man got up and went home. When the crowd saw this, they were filled with awe; and they praised God, who had given such authority to men.

Digging Deeper

- What was the kindness that the men showed to their friend in verse 2? Why was that kind?
- What was the kindness that Jesus showed the man in verse 2? Why was that kind?
- Jesus showed the man another kindness in verse 6. What happened when the crowds saw that kindness?
- What is the act of kindness that Jesus has shown you?
- Read 1 John 3:18. What is a way that you can show love by an act of kindness to someone?

Let's Pray

Dear Lord, thank you for being so kind to us. We love to read in the Bible of how you healed people and were so kind to them by providing them with all that they needed even when it seems impossible to us. And today we thank you for the biggest kindness you have shown – giving your life on the cross so that sinners might believe in you and have eternal life with you.

Please forgive me for the times when I have been unkind, and help me to be like you by showing acts of kindness even though it might be hard.

In Jesus' name,

Amen

Our God is a Kind God

GOD'S WORD: PSALM 86:1-7

David, who wrote this Psalm, knew that God was interested in his life. That's why he wrote this song, crying out to God when he was feeling distressed and anxious.

Let's Read
Turn in your Bible to Psalm 86:1-7

Hear, O LORD, and answer me, for I am poor and needy. Guard my life, for I am devoted to you. You are my God; save your servant who trusts in you. Have mercy on me, Oh Lord, for I call to you all day long.

Bring joy to your servant, for to you O Lord, I lift up my soul. You are forgiving and good, O Lord, abounding in love to all who call to you.

Hear my prayer, O LORD; listen to my cry for mercy. In the day of trouble I will call to you, for you will answer me.

God is interested in the details of our lives: the small things and the not so small things; the things that give us joy and happiness; the things that cause us to feel anxious or scared; the things that are important to us, the dreams and plans that we hold near to our hearts. Even things that might seem silly – such as when we feel sad because we're not going to spend our summer vacation with our friends, or when we have lost something precious to us.

David knew that God was interested in his life. As we know, David was not liked by everyone and some people wanted to harm him, but David knew that nothing could happen to him unless God allowed it. David asked God to guard his life. He reminded himself that God forgave sin, is good and is kind.

Do you remember God's kindness to you when you are anxious or scared? Do you remember that God sent His only Son Jesus so that your sins might be forgiven and that you might have a personal relationship with Him? God has given His Holy Spirit to those who believe in Him to be a guide and help. Remember the blessings that God has given you – your family, your friends, all the wonderful things you enjoy? Isn't God a kind God?

24

Digging Deeper

- From Psalm 86:1-7 what are some of the ways in which David knows that God shows His kindness?

- David knew that God would answer his prayer (see verse 7). But sometimes the answer God gives is not what we have asked for. For example, He might not give us what we want in order that we can learn to be thankful for what we have. Is God still kind if that happens? How is God still kind?

- One of the ways God shows His kindness to us is through forgiving our sins. How can we have our sins forgiven? Can you think of any verses in the Bible which tell you how you can have your sins forgiven? (Look up 1 John 1:9)

- David knew that God was kind and so he cried out to God in his distress. The Bible tells us that when we tell God all that we are upset about, we will know His peace.

- Read Philippians 4:6-7. Are there things that you feel worried or anxious about that you need to pray about? Write out that prayer now.

Let's Pray

Dear Father, we are so thankful for the kindness that you showed to David and that you show to us. We thank you that you sent your Son Jesus to die for our sins that we might be forgiven. We thank you that you care about every part of our lives and that you are in control. We ask you to forgive us for the times that we are ungrateful. Please help us to be kind to others as you are kind to us.

In Jesus' name,

Amen

Love Does Not Envy

GOD'S WORD: 1 CORINTHIANS 13:4-7

Do you know what it is to envy someone? Envy has been defined as a feeling of discontentedness and resentment caused by a desire for the possessions or qualities of someone else. Can you think of a time when you have been envious?

I remember a time when I was about seven. There was a girl in my class who was an only child. She was spoilt and, to be honest, it was pretty hard to like her because she was someone who liked to boast about all the cool things she had. It didn't really bother me too much though until she came to school one day and told us that in the next school break, her parents were taking her to Disneyland. Disneyland! Not only did she get to go to Disneyland, but she would have to go on a plane to get there! Oh, my heart just filled with envy. I loved to fly, and I wanted so much to go to

Disneyland. I had seen it on TV – kids standing next to Mickey Mouse, the neat rides, the fairy castle, the fireworks. Oh boy, did my heart hurt to know that SHE was going – and I wasn't. I went home and I complained. And complained. And complained. But did that get me to Disneyland? Nope, it just made me and everyone else in my house miserable. I don't remember if she actually went or not – but I still remember very clearly how miserable and sorry for myself I felt.

Let me tell you another story about someone who was miserable in their envy of someone.

Let's Read
Turn in your Bible to 1 Samuel 18:6-9

When the men were returning home after David had killed the Philistine, the women came out from all the towns of Israel to meet King Saul with singing and dancing, with joyful songs and with tambourines and lutes. As they danced, they sang: 'Saul has slain his thousands, and David his tens of thousands.'

This is an account of King Saul and the young David. David had killed Goliath and was becoming more and more important in the king's army because the Lord was blessing David and all that he did. What happened in 1 Samuel 18: 6–9?

28

King Saul and his army were returning from war. The people were so excited to have them home that they came out and literally had a party on the road to welcome the men home. King Saul's army had won a victory, and the people were even singing about how many people Saul had killed.

But there was a problem. David had killed more people and King Saul felt jealous. To make matters worse, the people also knew that David had killed more, and so that increased the king's jealousy still further. Verse 9 says, 'And from that time on Saul kept a jealous eye on David.'

King Saul had a choice to make. He could either be grateful for David and his help, or he could feel jealous of David and feel sorry for himself. Saul chose to feel jealous and envious. In choosing jealousy Saul began to hate David. Even though David was loyal to the king, Saul hated him. Then Saul began to look for opportunities to take David's life.

Jealousy or envy might only seem like a small sin — but we see in this story how it took over Saul's heart and mind and instead of loving David as a loyal servant, Saul instead chose to hate him. Sadly, Saul never did give up that jealousy of David and over the years there were many times when Saul tried to end David's life. However,

29

God protected David from this wicked man. God loved David and in His Word we are reminded that 'Love does not envy'.

Digging Deeper

- King Saul had a son called Jonathan. Read 1 Samuel 18:1-4. What did Jonathan feel towards David? What did he do to show that?
- Why do you think that Saul felt envy towards David?
- Read 1 Samuel 24:1-7. How did David treat Saul even though he knew Saul wanted to kill him? Why do you think David acted in this way?
- Think of a time when you have been envious of someone – maybe that person had something that you wanted, or maybe they were better than you at something. Has this changed? How can you show them love? Have you behaved kindly or unkindly towards them?
- Think about David's response to Saul.
- What could we choose instead of envy?

Let's Pray

*D*ear Father, sometimes I know I am envious of others, but I also know that it is not what you want me to be. Please forgive me when I am jealous and instead help me to choose to rejoice over the good things that others have or do.

I want to be someone who honours you by loving people and not being envious. Please help me in that.

In Jesus' name,
Amen

Stop Being Jealous!

GOD'S WORD: PSALM 37:3

ven when we have put our faith in God, sometimes we wish that we were living like those who do not love God. But the Bible tells us that this is wrong.

When you become a Christian the Holy Spirit enters your life to be your helper, but He doesn't take control and make you a robot. Because we were born sinners we will be sinners until we die, so there are times when our own hearts will be in a battle. We will know what the right thing is to do, but we might want to do the wrong thing. That wrong thing might seem more fun or easier. Sometimes we will look at others who choose to sin and wish we could do the same. It's good to realise that God knows the battle that we face. He tells us 'do not be envious of those who do wrong' because He knows sometimes we will be.

Maybe you are in class or in church and there are some kids who are messing around. They are whispering and giggling and passing notes. Oh, it looks so fun and you wish you could join in, except that you know it would be wrong. It would be disrespectful to your teacher or pastor and it would be distracting to others who are trying to concentrate. It would be sin; sin that Jesus paid the price for with His own life. It's that serious.

Psalm 37:3 tells us what to do instead.

Let's Read
Turn in your Bible to Psalm 37:1-3

o not fret because of evil men or be envious of those who do wrong; for like the grass they will soon wither, like green plants they will soon die away. Trust in the LORD and do good; dwell in the land and enjoy safe pasture.

Trust Him. Trust that when you do the right thing you actually honour the Lord and bless others. Do what is right because you know that it's the right thing to do. And tell your heart to stop being so jealous!

Digging Deeper

- When have you been jealous of someone who was doing something wrong? How did your heart feel? What were you thinking? What did you do? What was the best thing to do? Why?
- What do you think it means to 'dwell in the land and enjoy safe pasture'?
- To dwell in the land and enjoy safe pasture means to stay near to God by obeying Him. When you sin you move away from God and His will and you put your trust in yourself. That's not a good place to be. Sometimes we make decisions that are foolish and have long-lasting consequences. If we stay close to God by honouring and obeying Him in all that we do, then we are on safe ground.

Let's Pray

Dear God, thank you for knowing my heart and for knowing the things that I struggle with before I even know it myself. You are my Creator and by the work of your hands I am fearfully and wonderfully made. But sometimes I struggle to want to do the right thing and I need your

help. Please forgive me for the times I have
followed my own heart instead of following you
and please help me to choose what is best.

In Jesus' name,

Amen

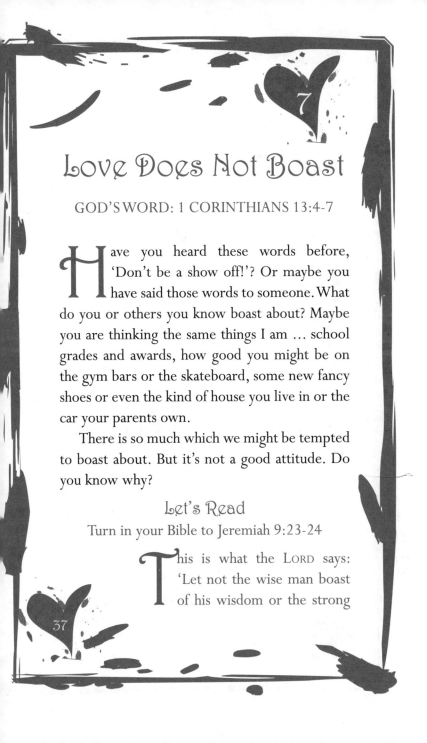

Love Does Not Boast

GOD'S WORD: 1 CORINTHIANS 13:4-7

Have you heard these words before, 'Don't be a show off!'? Or maybe you have said those words to someone. What do you or others you know boast about? Maybe you are thinking the same things I am … school grades and awards, how good you might be on the gym bars or the skateboard, some new fancy shoes or even the kind of house you live in or the car your parents own.

There is so much which we might be tempted to boast about. But it's not a good attitude. Do you know why?

Let's Read
Turn in your Bible to Jeremiah 9:23-24

This is what the LORD says: 'Let not the wise man boast of his wisdom or the strong man boast of his strength or the rich man boast of his riches, but let him who boasts boast about this: that he understands and knows me, that I am the LORD, who exercises kindness, justice and righteousness on earth, for in these things I delight' declares the LORD.

Read Ephesians 2:8-9

For it is by grace you have been saved, through faith – and this not of yourselves, it is the gift of God – not by works, so that no one can boast.

The Lord wants us to boast of nothing except Him. Even when we boast about knowing God, or about being a Christian, we cannot boast because we haven't done anything.

Ephesians 2:8-9 reminds us that we can't boast about being saved because God saved us. Salvation is a gift.

Doesn't that seem strange? God, through His Word, the Bible, tells us that the only thing that we can boast about is being saved – but then we can't boast about that because God saved us!

We didn't and couldn't save ourselves. So really all we can boast about is having a wonderful God who is able to save us. There is nothing left for us to boast about, is there?

So … don't be a show-off!

Let's Read
Turn in your Bible to Philippians 2:3-8

*D*o nothing out of selfish ambition or vain conceit, but in humility consider others better than yourselves. Each of you should look not only to your own interests, but also to the interests of others. Your attitude should be the same as that of Christ Jesus: Who, being in very nature God, did not consider equality with God something to be grasped, but made Himself nothing, taking the very nature of a servant, being made in human likeness. And being found in appearance as a man, He humbled Himself and became obedient to death – even death on a cross!

Digging Deeper

- Instead of a boastful attitude, what attitude should we have?
- What does humility mean? (You might want to ask an adult about this, or look it up in your dictionary).

39

- How did Jesus show humility?
- In what ways can we be humble as we follow Jesus' example?

Let's Pray

Dear God, sometimes I know I am a show-off and I ask you to forgive me. I don't want to cause others to be hurt or to be envious because of my own sin. Sometimes it is so hard to let someone else have the attention when I want it – but I know that is what it means to be humble. Help me to be humble just as Jesus was humble when He was on the earth. And help me to remember that everything I am good at is because you have given me the ability to do it.

In Jesus' name,

Amen

Our Great God

GOD'S WORD: PSALM 24:1-2

When God made the earth he SPOKE it into being. He said, 'Let it be' – and it was! Can you imagine! Wouldn't it be cool if we could walk into the kitchen and say, 'Let there be fresh cookies' – and they appeared on a plate! But we can't do that. Why? Because God is the only one who has the power to speak something into being. When God made us – His creation – He made us in His image, but not as a copy of Himself.

What does it mean that God made us in His image? Well, it means that there are qualities in us that are similar to qualities that God has.

Just as God is a being who loves to be in a relationship with people, He made us also to have relationships with others, but more especially with God Himself.

God made us to have friends, to enjoy other people's company, their sense of humour and their personalities. God gave us the ability to love and feel compassion and sympathy. He made us able to think and create and to dream. He gave us minds that love beauty and joy.

How do you think God knows all about these things? Because He Himself loves deeply. He created humour and enjoys creation and beauty. He weeps and has compassion and sympathy. We are made in the image of God.

Did you ever think God could have a sense of humour? Think about some of His creation. Do you think that God might enjoy watching tiger cubs roll about play-fighting? Maybe you think God doesn't care about the little things in life, but we can see that God cares for the animals because he gave many the ability to store up fat in their bodies in order to hibernate throughout the winter.

So God does care! God knows and God loves. Can we do any of this? Do we have the Might and Power of God to be able to order creation and tell the animals how they are to live? No. But we have the ability to know God and to live for Him, not because of anything that we have done – but because He made us that way.

42

Let's Read
Turn in your Bible to John 1: 19-27

Now this was John's testimony when the Jews of Jerusalem sent priests and Levites to ask him who he was. He did not fail to confess, but confessed freely, 'I am not the Christ.' They asked him, 'Then who are you? Are you Elijah?' He said, 'I am not.' 'Are you the Prophet?' He answered, 'No.' Finally they said, 'Who are you? Give us an answer to take back to those who sent us. What do you say about yourself?' John replied in the words of Isaiah the prophet, 'I am the voice of one calling in the desert, "Make straight the way for the Lord."' Now, some Pharisees who had been sent questioned him, 'Why then do you baptize if you are not the Christ, nor Elijah, nor the Prophet?' 'I baptize with water,' John replied, 'but among you stands one you do not know. He is the one who comes after me, the thongs of whose sandals I am not worthy to untie.'

John the Baptist was Jesus' cousin. He was also a man used by God to prepare the way for Jesus to come. He preached to the people and told them the

Saviour was coming and they needed to repent of their sin and be baptized.

Many thought John was the Messiah. They thought he was more important than a mere man. But John told them that Jesus was the Lamb of God, the promised Messiah and that he was not worthy of even untying Jesus' sandals.

John was humble. He knew that God had given him an important job to do, but he also knew that he had nothing to boast about. John did not expect people to treat him as more important than anyone else. John did not live in a fancy house with many servants. In fact he lived in the desert and ate locusts and honey! John was humble and he gave all the glory and honour to Jesus.

Digging Deeper

- Why was the job that John had so important?
- Was John more important to God than you or I are? Why or why not?
- God loves all of His people equally. He created them with different jobs to do – and gives each person the ability to do those jobs when they depend on Him. If God gives you a job and then gives you the ability to do it, would it be right to be boastful to others about how great you are?

44

- Make a list of the gifts and abilities that God has given you. Thank Him and ask Him to help you to use those talents to honour Him

Let's Pray

*D*ear Father, thank you for your wonderful creation. You made the beautiful things and the funny things and the amazing things – all with your might and power. You thought of everything from the snow on the mountains to the dots on the ladybirds. And you made us in your image to do the work that you would have for us. Help us to do that work well so that it shows others how great you are. Help us to remember that all that we can do and all that we are is because you are a great God.

In Jesus' name,

Amen

Love is Not Proud

GOD'S WORD: 1 CORINTHIANS 13:4-7

There was once a kingdom in a far-away land where there ruled a kind and wise king, and beside him his only son. This son, Prince Casper, was a spoilt child of eighteen and it came about that after much pampering and getting his own way, the young prince's heart overflowed with pride and selfishness.

Now all kings, queens, princes and princesses have a job to do. They must guard and protect, care for and love the people in their kingdom. But Casper thought that his job was to have others serve him and make his life as easy as possible. So spoilt and full of pride was this naughty prince that he refused to attend important banquets, meetings or events unless he felt like it!

His father, the king, was saddened by his son's foolish behaviour and decided one day to teach him what it is to humble oneself and become a servant. He dressed in

47

the uniform of the Palace Guard and accompanied the prince on a morning ride.

They had not gone far from the palace when the horses became skittish. They had sensed that something was wrong. The guards surrounded the Prince ready to protect him if they came under attack. The nerves of the horses proved correct. Within seconds the palace group was ambushed. The highway robbers came charging out of the woods with their guns and the fight was on!

In a short time the Palace Guards had fought off the attackers, but not without casualties. The prince had not noticed that one of the guards lay still on the ground until he heard the guard call his name. It was his father! The prince rushed to his father's side frightened and shaking. The guards carried the king back to the palace where the doctor was able to attend to save his life.

Prince Casper was so ashamed and remorseful. His eyes were opened to his selfish ways and his heart filled with grief that his father could have lost his life trying to teach his son a lesson. From that day on he resolved that he would no longer be Prince Casper the selfish, but Prince Casper the people's servant. Never again did he think more highly of himself than he ought.

48

Let's Read

Turn in your Bible to Matthew 6:5-6

And when you pray, do not be like the hypocrites, for they love to pray standing in the synagogues and on the street corners to be seen by men. I tell you the truth, they have received their reward in full. But when you pray, go into your room, close the door and pray to your Father, who is unseen. Then your Father, who sees what is done in secret, will reward you.

Read Romans 12:3

For by the grace given me I say to every one of you: Do not think of yourself more highly than you ought, but rather think of yourself with sober judgment, in accordance with the measure of faith God has given you.

Digging Deeper

- A hypocrite is someone who puts on an act, whose behaviour is different from what she really is. That means that a hypocrite's behaviour is not genuine.
- Why would we want other people to hear our prayers?
- It is not wrong for others to hear our prayers – but it is wrong for

49

us to want them to hear how wonderful we are at praying, or the big words we use. That is called pride. Pride is when we think too highly of ourselves.

- It is also wrong not to want to pray because you don't know the big words to say. That is also called pride because you want people to think that you are better than you really are.
- What things can we do to teach our hearts to be humble and not full of pride?
- What does it mean to think more highly of yourself than you ought?
- Another way to say, 'Do not think more highly of yourself than you ought,' is to say, 'Be humble'. What does 'be humble' mean?
- Which things out of this list describe someone who is humble?

They take the biggest piece of pie.
They boast about how good they are at singing.
They show off whenever they have guests over.
They put the needs of others before their own.
They encourage others for trying their hardest.

They get sulky when no-one notices them.
They love others even after they have been hurt by
them.

• Jesus is our greatest example of humility. What did Jesus do that showed He was humble?

Let's Pray

Dear Lord, thank you that you are the best example of being humble. Please forgive me for the times that I have behaved with pride and selfishness like the prince in our story. Please help me to put others first because I know that is what you do. I want others to know that I love you because of the way that I love them.

In your name, Jesus,
Amen

51

The Humble Heart

GOD'S WORD: PSALM 131:1

Where in your body is your heart? It's almost in the middle of your chest – just left a little. Put your hand over your heart and sit very still. Can you feel anything? Probably not. If you were to put your ear to someone's chest you would certainly hear a LOUD 'thump, thump'. Maybe you could try that now – is there someone sitting next to you?

What else would you hear if you put your ear to someone's chest? Would you hear if that person's heart were proud? No. Why not? Well, when the Bible talks about the heart, it is really referring to the mind. Your mind is the place where all your thoughts and feelings are.

When the writer of this Psalm speaks of his heart not being proud, he really means that he does not think of himself as more important or better than he really is. He says that he just sticks with the things that he should be doing – and does not consider himself an expert in areas into which he has no business sticking his nose.

I wonder if you have been tempted to do that. I know I have. Maybe there have been times when your parents have been talking about something and you have interrupted them because you think you know better. What kind of attitude do you think that shows in your heart?

Or how about when your younger brother or sister can't keep up with you and you get really annoyed. Does that show a proud attitude? Remember, pride is when you place yourself first because you think or know that you are better.

Let's look together at someone who was not proud – in fact He was the most humble person ever. Jesus and His disciples had gathered together for an evening meal …

Let's Read
Turn in your Bible to John 13:2-5

The evening meal was being served, and the devil had already prompted Judas Iscariot, son of Simon, to betray Jesus. Jesus knew that the Father had put all things under His power, and that He had come from God and was returning to God; so He

54

got up from the meal, took off His outer clothing, and wrapped a towel around His waist. After that He poured water into a basin and began to wash His disciples' feet, drying them with the towel that was wrapped round Him.

Do you wash the feet of people who come to your home for a meal? Or if you meet friends at a restaurant for dinner, do you all wash your feet first? No, I didn't think so! Why did Jesus wash His friends' feet then?

Let me tell you. In Jesus' day, there were no cars and no roads – well, not roads as we know them. There were dusty walk-ways and it wasn't just people that used them – donkeys, camels, cattle, dogs, all sorts of animals used them as well. We all know that these animals aren't toilet-trained – they just 'go' where they are. Picture what it would have been like to walk on these roads without proper walking boots. Jesus just had sandals. Some people probably didn't even have sandals – they would have walked barefoot. Not only would their feet have been dirty; they would probably also have been stinky!

So when Jesus and His disciples had met together for a meal they would have walked there. The meal was about to be served to them as they lay around the low table on their low

55

cushions (they didn't sit on chairs at a table to eat, as we do). But they had dirty, stinky feet; not a pleasant situation to be in before dinner. So Jesus washed everyone's feet out of love for them.

Digging Deeper

- Why didn't one of the disciples organise water for everyone to wash his own feet?
- Turn to Luke 9:46-48. Were the disciples proud or were they humble?
- When Jesus washed everyone's feet He made Himself a servant to them. Read Philippians 2:5-11. In what other way did Jesus humble Himself and become a servant?
- What does Philippians 2:5 say? How can your attitude be the same as Jesus?
- God exalts those who humble themselves. What are some ways that you can show a humble attitude to your parents/siblings/ friends/teachers?

Let's Pray

Dear Lord, thank you for the example that you have shown to us of being humble. When you washed the disciples' feet you were showing them that you loved them because you did not see yourself as more important than they were – even though you are the Son of God. And when you died on the cross you humbled yourself so that I could believe in you and receive eternal life. Please forgive me for the times that I have been proud. Help me to be humble just as you showed us.

In your name, Jesus,

Amen.

Love is Not Rude

GOD'S WORD: 1 CORINTHIANS 13:4-7

Are you ever told to 'mind your manners'? Let's see what manners we can think of. How about 'remember to say please and thank you'; 'don't speak with your mouth full'; 'don't interrupt a conversation'; 'remember to wash your hands before dinner'? Those are some of the good manner rules in our house. I wonder if you have any different rules in your house? I heard in some countries it is good manners to belch loudly at the end of the meal to show how much you enjoyed it (that is definitely not okay in our house)! How about this one for school teachers in New Zealand in the early 1900s —'You must not loiter (hang out) in downtown ice cream stores'. That seems funny to me!

Manners can seem funny and at times we don't understand their importance. But showing good manners towards people is a way of showing our love for them.

Imagine this: your mum has made your favourite dinner for your birthday to show you how much she loves you.

Before your family is seated at the table, you grab the biggest bread roll. You lift a heaped spoon of spaghetti and pile it on your plate, dribbling a lot of it all over the clean table-cloth.

You reach for the salad and knock the jug of juice over the bread rolls so now there are no bread rolls and no juice for anyone else.

All through dinner you talk loudly with your mouth full and no one else can get a word in edgeways!

After dinner your birthday cake is placed in front of you. You know your mum has tried so hard and she was up very late trying to make the cake you wanted – but you can't actually tell if it is a dog or a horse. You laugh and say 'What is this?'

At this point your father asks you to stand and join him in the other room. Uh oh. You are in trouble. Big trouble. But why? It's your birthday and you were just having some fun, right?

Wrong. You were enjoying yourself at the expense of others and that is rude. Love is not rude.

Let's Read

Turn in your Bible to Matthew 19: 16-22

Now a man came to Jesus and asked, 'Teacher, what good thing must I do to get eternal life?' 'Why do you ask me about what is good? Jesus replied. 'There is only One who is good. If you want to enter life, obey the commandments.' 'Which ones?' the man inquired. Jesus replied, '"Do not murder, do not commit adultery, do not steal, do not give false testimony, honor your father and mother," and "love your neighbor as yourself."' 'All these I have kept,' the young man said. 'What do I still lack?' Jesus answered, 'If you want to be perfect, go, sell your possessions and give to the poor, and you will have treasure in heaven. Then come, follow me.' When the young man heard this he went away sad, because he had great wealth.

Digging Deeper

- Read Matthew 19:19b. What does this verse mean?
- To love your neighbour as you love yourself means that we already love ourselves and that is how we are to love others. Some of the ways that we love ourselves are: feeding our bodies, keeping fit, spending time with those who make us feel happy. What are some other

things which we do that shows how much we love ourselves?

- We show others our love by behaving in a way that is not rude. We are to care for them and encourage them in what they are doing. What else can you do to show your love for others?

- Think back over the last few days. Have you shown rude behaviour? Perhaps you need to ask forgiveness for this and for not showing love as you should. Then remind yourself to STOP and CHANGE direction.

- Write Matthew 19:19b on a card and put it somewhere you can see it each day. Why would being reminded of this verse every day be helpful to you?

Let's Pray

Dear God, thank you for the different ways that I am learning to love people. I pray that you would help me to learn and remember good manners so that I can show love to others in the way that I behave towards them. Please forgive me for the times when I have been rude and help me to ask for forgiveness from those I have been rude to. Please help me to love others just as much as I love myself.

In Jesus' name, Amen.

Be a Good Neighbour

GOD'S WORD: PSALM 133:1

Did you know that when we get on with each other and love each other as we should, this honours and pleases God? The flip-side is the opposite of that – if we do not get on with each other it dishonours and saddens God.

The Bible speaks a lot to us about unity. Do you know what unity is? Unity is when we agree with one another and can be together at school, home or in the playground without arguing or fighting.

Think about when you are at home or school and there is a fight that starts between two kids. There is yelling and noise and sometimes there might be pushing and even hitting. Is there anything pleasant about that? Do parents or teachers say, 'Oh, how wonderful! The children are fighting! How that makes my heart sing with joy!'

Hardly! Why not? Well, let's think about what happens when people don't get along. They are often unkind to one another. They might say rude and mean things. They cannot get things done together because they are so cross that they don't even want to agree on anything. Then it starts to rub off on those around them as they show their bad attitudes, selfish and rude behaviour and a sad lack of love. No love?! That's right. If love is patient and kind, not self-seeking and definitely not rude, then fighting and arguing is unloving.

Let's Read
Turn in your Bible to 1 Corinthians 12:14-18

The body is not made up of one part but of many. If the foot should say, 'Because I am not a hand, I do not belong to the body,' it would not for that reason cease to be part of the body. And if the ear should say, 'Because I am not an eye, I do not belong to the body,' it would not for that reason cease to be part of the body. If the whole body were an eye, where would the sense of hearing be? If the whole body were an ear, where would the sense of smell be? But in fact God has arranged the parts in the body, every one of them, just as He wanted them to be.

The Apostle Paul is writing to the Corinthian church and wants to talk to them about being united. He is writing about spiritual gifts. A spiritual gift is something the Holy Spirit gives you when you become a Christian – but it's a gift with a difference. These gifts are not something you can see, like a new bike or a Christmas present, but is God's special help to enable you to serve others in a specific way.

For example, some have the gift of being able to teach the Bible in a clear way that enables people to understand it. Some people have the gift of being merciful which means that they can help people in ways that some of us might not think to do or be able to do. Others might have a special gift of giving money or of having great wisdom to enable them to help others to make wise decisions.

You see, the spiritual gift that you have is not for your benefit, but to benefit others. Ask your parents or Pastor if you want to find out more about spiritual gifts.

There is not one gift that is more important, as all are needed. But the Christians in the Corinthian church thought there were some gifts that were more important and so those were the gifts they wanted. Paul needed to

65

remind them that a church requires all sorts of people with all sorts of gifts to serve in the many different ways that a church needs.

If the church was full of people who could only give money, who would teach the Bible or look after the elderly and the sick, or help those in difficult situations who need great wisdom?

Paul wrote that all gifts are valuable. They can be ways of showing love to one another because they are all about serving one another. Paul wanted the Corinthians to be glad about the different ways they could show love to one another and to stop disagreeing about which was the most important!

Digging Deeper

- When we don't agree with someone we have a choice to make. We can choose to treat them badly because we think they are wrong – or we can choose to love them and show them respect. We can ask God to help us find a solution. Which is the best decision?

- What happens when people can't agree on something and they respond rudely to one another? Do they love one another or do they love themselves more?

- When you are arguing with someone, do you think you are available to God to serve others? Why or why not?
- Does fighting over something show good manners or rude manners?
- What can we do to fix a situation where we don't get on with someone because there is something we don't agree about?
- Here are some thoughts: We can seek forgiveness for a wrong attitude or behaviour. We can pray and ask God for wisdom to know what is right. We can choose to keep loving the person as we love ourselves. We can go to someone older or wiser than we are and ask for help.

Let's Pray

Dear Lord, I want to be the kind of person who honours you by the way I love others. Please help me to love others and to try my best not to argue. Please give me wisdom for the times when I don't agree with others so that I can show them love while we come to a solution.

In Jesus' name,
Amen

67

Love is Not Self-Seeking

GOD'S WORD: 1 CORINTHIANS 13:4-7

Self-seeking. That is a funny phrase, isn't it? Do you think it means that you are looking for yourself?

No – how can you look for yourself! Even when you close your eyes you are still seeing you (even the backs of your eyelids count as you). But if we put the word 'out' in our definition then we might be closer to understanding what it means to be self-seeking.

Self-seeking means that you look out for yourself. You make sure that you are the first in line, that you get the biggest cookie on the plate, the best seat on the sofa. That's self-seeking. We're all pretty good at being self-seeking – but the problem is, love is not self-seeking.

Now, in the next reading the Apostle Paul is writing of some of his experiences as a missionary.

69

Let's Read

Turn in your Bible to 2 Corinthians 11:23b-27

I have worked much harder, been in prison more frequently, been flogged more severely, and been exposed to death again and again. Five times I received from the Jews the forty lashes minus one. Three times I was beaten with rods, once I was stoned, three times I was shipwrecked, I spent a night and a day in the open sea, I have been constantly on the move. I have been in danger from rivers, in danger from bandits, in danger from my own countrymen, in danger from Gentiles; in danger in the city, in danger in the country, in danger at sea; and in danger from false brothers. I have laboured and toiled and have often gone without sleep; I have known hunger and thirst and have often gone without food; I have been cold and naked.

Wow. That sounds like Paul was playing a video game and playing it very badly! Except that it wasn't a game. And all these things that Paul writes about actually happened. Paul was a missionary. He was someone who loved Jesus and shared the good news of salvation with as many people as he

70

could. We know Paul as a great apostle of Jesus Christ. Paul is someone whom we admire and respect. But in his day Paul was often hated and ridiculed. He nearly lost his life many times and eventually he was killed for being a missionary of Jesus Christ. Do you think Paul was self-seeking? There is one who suffered even more than Paul …

Let's Read
Turn in your Bible to Matthew 27:27-38

Then the governor's soldiers took Jesus into the Praetorium and gathered the whole company of soldiers around Him. They stripped Him and put a scarlet robe on Him, and then twisted together a crown of thorns and set it on His head. They put a staff in His right hand and knelt in front of Him and mocked Him. 'Hail, king of the Jews!' they said. They spit on Him, and took the staff and struck Him on the head again and again. After they had mocked Him, they took off the robe and put His own clothes on Him. Then they led Him away to crucify Him. As they were going out, they met a man from Cyrene, named Simon, and they forced him to carry the cross. They came to a place called Golgotha (which

71

means The Place of the Skull). There they offered Jesus wine to drink, mixed with gall; but after tasting it, He refused to drink it. When they had crucified Him, they divided up His clothes by casting lots. And sitting down, they kept watch over Him there. Above His head they placed the written charge against Him: THIS IS JESUS, THE KING OF THE JEWS. Two robbers were crucified with Him, one on His right and one on His left.

Turn in you Bible to John 3:16

For God so loved the world that He gave His one and only Son, that whoever believes in Him shall not perish but have eternal life.

Digging Deeper

- Why did Christ allow Himself to be crucified?
- Did it hurt Jesus to wear a crown of thorns? Would it have hurt Him to be flogged and then nailed to a cross and crucified? Did Jesus deserve any of what He suffered? Why or why not?

- Read 1 John 3:16 How do we know that Jesus loved us?
- Jesus was not self-seeking. He left His throne and the glory of Heaven to come to this earth as a man so He could die for our sins. The opposite of being self-seeking is to be selfless. This means that you consider your own comfort and needs to be less important than anyone else's.
- What are three things that you could do to show a selfless heart today?
- If love is not self-seeking, it must be self_____

Let's Pray

Dear God, thank you for the example that Jesus is to us of being selfless. When He laid down His life and died for us so that we can be forgiven, He showed that He loved us more than He loved Himself. Please forgive me for the times when I have been selfish. Please help me to be selfless and to love others more than I love myself.

In Jesus' name,
Amen.

Fruit in Your Heart

GOD'S WORD: PSALM 66:1-4

When you make sure that your heart (mind) is focused on God and what He has done for us, it is very hard to be self- seeking. Remember being self-seeking is looking out for ourselves first. Do you think that the writer of Psalm 66 was trying to make himself look good? Did he want people to say, 'Oh, wow – you are such a great writer! I could never write anything in the way that you do!'

No! He was wanting people to focus on God's greatness. This shows that the psalmist had a humble heart towards God and that he served God before he served himself.

Let's Read
Turn in your Bible to Luke 6:45b

For out of the overflow of his (a man's) heart his mouth speaks.'

Turn in your Bible to Luke 6:43-45

No good tree bears bad fruit, nor does a bad tree bear good fruit. Each tree is recognised by its own fruit. People do not pick figs from thorn-bushes, or grapes from briers. The good man brings good things out of the good stored up in his heart, and the evil man brings evil things out of the evil stored up in his heart. For out of the overflow of his heart his mouth speaks.

Digging Deeper

- Think about what Luke 6:45b means.
- If a good apple tree produces or bears good apples, what 'fruit' does a heart produce?
- When we talk about fruit in a person's life we are talking about the things which show us whether or not they love Jesus and others.
- Turn to Galatians 5:22-23. What nine fruit are listed there?
- Look back at Luke 6:45. If a Christian has the fruit listed in Galatians, should we hear him speak things that are unkind or untrue? What should they speak instead?

- 'For out of the overflow of the heart, the mouth speaks.' If we have joy in our heart our words will be joyful. If we have peace in our hearts our words and actions will be calm. If we have kindness in our hearts our words and actions will be …

- To have this fruit in our hearts, our hearts must belong to Jesus. We can ask Him to help our hearts grow good fruit. Does your heart belong to Jesus?

- What words have come out of your mouth lately? Kind words? True words? Gentle words? Or perhaps complaining words? Arguing words? What do your words say about what is in your heart? Are there things you need to put right with people because of your words?

Let's Pray

Dear God, how amazing that you have given us a way to tell if our hearts are bearing good or bad fruit – we only need to look at the words we speak and the way we behave. Please forgive me for the times I have spoken and behaved badly. Help me to put things right with those to whom I have spoken or behaved badly. I need your help to have a heart full of good fruit – so please help me.

In Jesus' name, Amen.

Not Easily Angered

GOD'S WORD: 1 CORINTHIANS 13:4-7

Sometimes when I was younger I would go into my bedroom and find one of my little brothers in my stuff. I would get so mad and yell 'GET OUT OF MY ROOM!' Then my brother would grab something of mine and run as fast as he could to Mum. I would be yelling 'MUM! HE HAS MY STUFF! MAKE HIM GIVE IT BACK!' Usually by this time he would be crying because my yelling had frightened him, but I didn't care. I was so angry!

Now my own girls have a little brother who does exactly the same thing. But let's find out what Jesus said to someone who got really angry ...

Let's Read
Turn in your Bible to Luke 22:47-51

While He was still speaking a crowd came up, and the man who was called

Judas, one of the Twelve, was leading them. He approached Jesus to kiss Him, but Jesus asked him, 'Judas, are you betraying the Son of Man with a kiss?' When Jesus' followers saw what was going to happen, they said, 'Lord, should we strike with our swords?' And one of them struck the servant of the high priest, cutting off his right ear. But Jesus answered, 'No more of this!' And He touched the man's ear and healed him.

Jesus was betrayed by Judas and then the soldiers came to arrest Him. Was it right that they arrested Him? No! Had Jesus done anything wrong? No! He was innocent. Judas, one of Jesus' disciples, had betrayed Jesus for a few silver coins.

Jesus knew that Judas was going to betray Him and yet He loved Judas and was His friend. Now Jesus was being taken by the soldiers and He knew that it would not be long before He was nailed to a cross to die a very painful death. However, Jesus wasn't angry. Peter was, though. Peter took his sword and swung it, but all he did was cut off a soldier's ear. That was not going to protect Jesus. So what did Jesus do? Well, Jesus knew that He had to die so He reached out and healed this man's ear and then He allowed the soldiers to take Him.

80

Even though He knew what Judas and these soldiers were going to do, He did not yell at them. No, Jesus showed love to sinners by going through this painful death on the cross. Jesus is love.

Let's Read
Turn in your Bible to James 1:19-20

My dear brothers, take note of this: Everyone should be quick to listen, slow to speak and slow to become angry, for man's anger does not bring about the righteous life that God desires.

Digging Deeper

- What things make you angry?
- When was the last time you were angry?
- What did you do to show you were angry?
- Was that right or wrong behaviour – in other words, did it show love to others?
- What is the best way to respond in a situation like that?
- Being slow to speak means that we should always think carefully about what we are going to say to make sure that our words are true, kind, gentle, patient and loving and necessary. I don't know about you, but

81

sometimes I say things and as soon as the words come out of my mouth I wish I hadn't said them. We all need to be slow to speak.

- What things can you do to make yourself slow to speak?
- What things can you do to make yourself slow to become angry?
- Jesus is the best example of someone who loves perfectly without becoming easily angered. How can we become more like Jesus?

Let's Pray

Dear God, thank you that even when I am angry, you love me. I know there are times when I am quick to become angry and I ask your forgiveness for that. Please help me to be self-controlled in my actions and words and to be selfless when I feel like being angry? Please help me to be more like your Son.

In Jesus' name,
Amen

Slow to Anger

GOD'S WORD: PSALM 86:11-15

*D*id you know that we can ask God to help us to be like Him and He will answer us? Isn't that wonderful?

Let's Read
Turn in your Bible to Psalm 86:11-15

*T*each me your way, O LORD, and I will walk in your truth; give me an undivided heart, that I may fear your name. I will praise you, O Lord my God, with all my heart; I will glorify your name forever. For great is your love toward me; you have delivered me from the depths of the grave. The arrogant are attacking me, O God; a band of ruthless men seeks my life – men without regard for you. But you, O Lord, are a compassionate and gracious God, slow to anger, abounding in love and faithfulness.

The writer of today's Psalm was David. He was the young shepherd boy who killed the giant Goliath and was eventually made King of Israel. But even David needed help to obey God and so he asked for God's help. Let's look at what David was asking for:

Verse 11. He wanted to know how to live so that he could make sure to obey and honour God with his life.

Verse 11b. David wanted an undivided heart. This means that he wanted to be totally committed to worshipping God. However, he knew that sometimes there were things which distracted him; things like riches, fame, and fear for his life. These things could all be a distraction for David if he didn't keep his mind totally focused on worshipping the Lord.

David wanted to praise the Lord with all of his heart and mind because he knew just how much God loved him and what God had done for him. God had saved David and David knew that when he died he would be with the Lord in heaven.

Digging Deeper

- Look at verse 14. David was in trouble. Men were after him and were trying to take his life. What does he mean when he says 'men without regard for you'?

- David goes on to write verse 15. He compares the men who want to kill him to God. What words does David use to describe God?

- What do each of the words David uses to describe God mean?

- Give an example of how you can be: compassionate; gracious; slow to anger; abounding in love; abounding in faithfulness.

- David so wanted to follow the Lord that he asked God to show him how to live a life that would please Him. How do we know what pleases God and how we should live?

- God has given us His Word, the Bible, to teach us about Him and give us instructions on how to live. Sometimes when we read the Bible it is hard to understand and we don't know what it means. At these times it is good to ask someone who knows the Bible for help. Perhaps you could ask your parents or pastor or Sunday School teacher.

85

- To whom can you go for help when you don't understand what you are reading in the Bible?

Let's Pray

Dear God, David loved you so much, but sometimes he still sinned and did not obey you. I want to love you like David – and so, just as David did, I want to ask that you help me to live a life that pleases you. Please help me to be compassionate and gracious and loving because I know that it honours you.

In Jesus' name,

Amen.

No Record of Wrongs

GOD'S WORD: 1 CORINTHIANS 13:4-7

How far is the east from the west? They are opposite directions, right?

If you were to look at a compass you would see that the compass points right to the east and left to the west. East and west will never meet each other.

Are you wondering what is so important about how far the east is from the west? It's because the Bible tells us that 'as far as the east is from the west, so far has He (God) removed our sins from us' (Psalm 103:12). That means that God keeps no record of our sin. When we ask Him to forgive us He not only forgives our sins, but chooses not to remember them any longer: 'For I will forgive their wickedness and will remember their sins no more' (Hebrews 8:12). Jesus paid for our sins so we don't need to do anything more than ask for forgiveness and God forgives and remembers them no more. Wow! So even when you are cheeky to your dad and you ask forgiveness for your bad attitude, your sin is forgiven and forgotten. And if your dad loves the Lord then his attitude towards you should also be the same – when you ask forgiveness he needs to both forgive and forget. That's what Christians are called to do.

How about you? What happens when someone is unkind towards you? When they ask your forgiveness, do you forgive and forget? Or do you say you forgive, but then keep it in your mind and still get angry and upset over it later? If that is what you do that is called 'keeping a record of wrongs'. That's not love.

Let's Read
Turn in your Bible to Matthew 18:21-22

Then Peter came to Jesus and asked, 'Lord, how many times shall I forgive my brother when he sins against me? Up to seven times?' Jesus answered, 'I tell you, not seven times, but seventy seven times.'

Peter was asking the Lord how often he should forgive those who do wrong towards him. He thought he was being very gracious in suggesting that he forgive someone seven times, but Jesus surprised Peter by saying that he

88

needed to forgive seventy seven times. In other words he needed to forgive many, many times – without limit.

Do you know how much seventy times seven is? 490! Could you keep count of how many times that someone wrongs you up to 490 times? You would have to write every time down so that you could remember it. Maybe it might look something like this:

Monday: He/she made fun of my laugh.

Tuesday: He/she stole my lunch.

Wednesday: He/she told lies about me.

Thursday: He/she pushed me over.

Friday: He/she said unkind things about my art work.

But there is a problem. We would be sinning if we did that. The Bible tells us that we are not to keep a record of wrongs. That's not love.

Digging Deeper

- Is there something you need to ask forgiveness for right now? Then ask Him to do so. How far has that sin been removed from you?
- Do you need to forgive someone?
- When we speak of forgiving and forgetting we don't literally mean forget. We can't choose

89

to wipe something from our memory. It means that we forgive that person and then we choose to keep forgiving them. We don't allow ourselves to think about it and become angry again. Every time we think about the wrong or hurt we suffered we straightaway choose to forgive them again and put it away from our thoughts. This is really hard to do sometimes and we need to ask God to help us with this.

- Do you need to ask God for help with that now?

Let's Pray

Dear God, when Jesus died on the cross for my sins that meant that I no longer needed to pay for my wrongdoing. Thank you that when I ask for forgiveness you forgive my sin and choose to remember it no more. You put my sin as far from me as the east is from the west. I am so grateful because I know that I have done nothing to deserve that.

Please help me to forgive others and to keep on forgiving them.

In Jesus' name,

Amen

Don't Forget!

GOD'S WORD: PSALM 103:1-2

While there are some things that it's important for us to forget (like the things we have forgiven others for), there are also some things that it's important to remember!

Do you know the saying, 'Don't take it for granted'? It means that sometimes we forget the wonderful things that we have in our lives and we behave in an ungrateful manner. We forget to be thankful. Can you think of things which you 'take for granted'?

Let me tell you about what I sometimes take for granted: good food to eat every day, a warm bed to sleep in, the nice things around me that I enjoy, books that I love to read, my family and friends who love me very much.

Do you take some of these things for granted too? Are you grateful for your family, the fun times you have, the food you eat? Do you remember to say thank you as often as you should? Or are there times when you say 'I'm bored' or 'I don't like eating that for dinner', or 'I've got nothing to wear'?

Each time you say things like that, it's because you have taken for granted the many blessings in your life, blessings that others will never enjoy.

If you ever complain about what is for dinner, remember that some people in the world don't have the privilege of a dinner to eat. It's easy to take something for granted and to be ungrateful. What are you thankful for right now?

Let's Read
Turn in your Bible to Psalm 103:1-5

Praise the LORD, O my soul; all my inmost being, praise His holy name. Praise the LORD, O my soul, and forget not all His benefits – who forgives all your sins and heals all your diseases, who redeems your life from the pit and crowns you with love and compassion, who satisfies your desires with good things so that your youth is renewed like the eagle's.

David wrote this Psalm reminding himself and us of all the wonderful things that the Lord had done for those who trust in Him. Let's look at those:

92

The Lord has forgiven sin.

The Lord heals diseases.

The Lord saves from death.

The Lord is loving and compassionate.

The Lord is generous and gives good things.

The Lord renews strength.

These are things for which we should all remember to be thankful. They are things that we should not take for granted.

Digging Deeper

- What else can you think of that you are thankful to the Lord for?
- What is a good way you can remind yourself to be thankful for the Lord's goodness to you?
- David was often in a situation where his life was in danger. Yet he was still able to be thankful to the Lord. Why do you think that is?
- When we are tempted to bear a grudge we should remember the good things that the Lord has done for us. Maybe you could make a list of things to be thankful to the Lord for and keep it next to your bed where you can read it regularly. What would be the first three things you would put on your 'thankful list'?

Let's Pray

Dear Lord, thank you for the example of David who reminds us not to take you for granted. You are so good to us and so kind. However, it can be hard to remember to be thankful all the time. But I know I need to be thankful because you are so caring and you love me very much.

Thank you for Jesus who died for my sins. Thank you for the family and friends who love me and that I have everything that I need and more. Thank you that you are patient and kind with me and that you continue to teach me from your Word even though I don't deserve your goodness. Please help me to have a thankful attitude towards you and others too.

In Jesus' name,

Amen.

Do Not Delight In Evil

GOD'S WORD: 1 CORINTHIANS 13:4-7

I wonder if you know the story of Queen Esther? Esther was a girl you can read about in your Bible. She was raised by her cousin Mordecai, a man who loved and feared God. God used Esther to save His chosen people, the Jews.

One day Esther was taken to the Palace where she was chosen to become Queen. Here she met one of the king's servants, a man named Haman. Haman was a wicked man who was full of love for himself. Haman loved to receive honour from people and he expected all the citizens of the city to bow and honour him whenever he walked past.

One day it was noted that Mordecai the Jew did not bow to Haman. Haman was furious and began to think of a way to kill Mordecai. When Haman realised that Mordecai was a Jew he became even more murderous in his heart and made a plan for all of God's chosen people to be killed. Haman deviously got the king's agreement to this wicked plan and was overjoyed. His heart was delighting in evil.

Did Haman succeed in his wicked plan? No. God used Mordecai and Esther to change the king's heart and Haman's plans were overthrown. However, Haman was repaid for his evil intentions and lost his life. Read more about this true story in the book of Esther in your Bible.

Let's Read

Turn in your Bible to 1 Peter 3:8-9

Finally, all of you, live in harmony with one another; be sympathetic, love as brothers, be compassionate and humble. Do not repay evil with evil or insult with insult, but with blessing, because to this you were called so that you may inherit a blessing.

Digging Deeper

- Haman's problem was that he was full of love for himself. According to 1 Peter 3:8-9, how should Haman have responded when Mordecai refused to bow to him?

96

- 1 Peter 3:9 says we should not repay evil with evil, or insult with insult, but with blessing. How could you bless someone if they spoke unkindly to you?

Let's Read
Turn in your Bible to 1 Peter 3:10-12

For, 'Whoever would love life and see good days must keep his tongue from evil and his lips from deceitful speech. He must turn from evil and do good; he must seek peace and pursue it. For the eyes of the Lord are on the righteous and his ears are attentive to their prayer, but the face of the Lord is against those who do evil.'

Digging Deeper

- Why is it so important to obey verse 8-9?
- Look at 1 Peter 3:12. Are 'the righteous' those who repay evil with evil and insult with insult? Or are they those who repay with a blessing? Who are the righteous?
- 'The righteous' are Christians because when Jesus died and paid for our sins He made us right with God. God now sees those who believe and trust in Him as righteous.
- Do you delight in evil? Or are you righteous?

97

Let's Pray

Dear Lord, the story of Esther is amazing because it reminds us that you are in control, and shows us that you will not honour those who delight in evil. Thank you for using Esther and Mordecai for overcoming evil. Please help me to be someone who delights in good. Give me courage to stand up for what is right.

In Jesus' name,
Amen

Don't Be a Fool!

GOD'S WORD: PSALM 53:1

Do you know what a missionary is? A missionary is a Christian who spends his or her life telling other people about God, so they too can believe and be saved. Some missionaries go overseas to another country. Some stay where they are. In fact ALL Christians are missionaries.

The Bible tells us in Matthew 28:19 to 'go and make disciples of all nations, baptising them in the name of the Father and of the Son and of the Holy Spirit, and teaching them to obey everything I have commanded you.'

We are all to obey this command and go and tell people about Jesus. But it's sometimes a difficult thing to do. Some people don't want to believe in God because they love to sin. They love the life that they live and don't want to obey anyone but themselves. If they were to believe in God they would have to turn from their sinful lives and live to honour God. So they say, 'There is no God!' Do you ever wonder how God deals with such people?

Let's Read
Turn in your Bible to Daniel 4:29-33

Twelve months later, as the king was walking on the roof of the royal palace of Babylon, he said, 'Is not this the great Babylon I have built as the royal residence, by my mighty power and for the glory of my majesty?' The words were still on his lips when a voice came from heaven, 'This is what is decreed for you, King Nebuchadnezzar: Your royal authority has been taken from you. You will be driven away from people and will live with the wild animals; you will eat grass like cattle. Seven times will pass by for you until you acknowledge that the Most High is sovereign over the kingdoms of men and gives them to anyone He wishes.' Immediately what had been said about Nebuchadnezzar was fulfilled. He was driven away from people and ate grass like cattle. His body was drenched with the dew of heaven until his hair grew like the feathers of an eagle and his nails like the claws of a bird.

100

So who was King Nebuchadnezzar? He was King of Babylon, a powerful nation, but his heart was full of pride and he chose not to believe in God.

One day the king had a frightening dream. He called in his magicians, astrologers and diviners—none of whom loved God. Not one of them could explain the meaning of the dream. The king then called for Daniel, a young man who worshipped the true God. Daniel told the king that the dream was a warning. God wanted the king to know that unless he turned from the sin in his life and worshipped the true God, he would lose his kingdom. The king refused. God had chosen to show compassion by giving Nebuchadnezzar time to repent. But he carried on as he was. Twelve months later he lost his kingdom and even worse, strange things happened to his body and mind, and he became like a wild animal.

Digging Deeper

- What was wrong with the king's words in verse 30?
- The king's words showed the fruit that was in his heart—the fruit of pride and love for himself instead of love for God. What happened to the king after he spoke these proud words?

101

- Why do you think God chose this way to teach the king about his sin? Nebuchadnezzar went from powerful king to being like a wild animal. Whose power did that display?
- Could even a powerful, mighty and rich king disregard God's commands for obedience? Why not?
- Read verse 34. How did Nebuchadnezzar respond? Was God honoured? Was Nebuchadnezzar still a fool in the eyes of God?
- How about you? Are you a fool who says, 'There is no God!'? Or are you wise, someone who desires with all their heart to honour and obey the true God?

Let's Pray

Dear God, even though you may not choose to humble a king in such a way today, I know that you still discipline and judge those who do not repent from their sin and turn to you. Please help me to reach out to others who do not know you and share the good news of your Son Jesus with them. Help me to be a missionary where I am so that people can turn from being fools to being wise. Help me to be wise also.

In Jesus' name,
Amen

Rejoice With the Truth

GOD'S WORD: 1 CORINTHIANS 13:4-7

Do you know what 'truth' is? Is it just whatever we think is right? Or is it what our parents or teachers or even the police tell us is right? Sometimes it is – as long as what they are saying is also what the Bible says.

Jesus said, 'I am the way, and the truth and the life' (John 14:6).

What did He mean that He is the truth? Isn't the truth a 'something' and not a 'someone'? Jesus was meaning that He is the way to God and that only by believing in Him can we be saved. Any other way we are told that we can become a Christian is not truth – it's a lie.

Knowing how to be saved from our sins and to receive eternal life with Jesus is the most important thing we can ever know. It doesn't matter how many books we have read or how many languages we can speak. It doesn't matter how many memory verses we know – if we don't know the truth about salvation all other knowledge is useless. Oh sure, it might help us to get a job or to get good grades. That's fine and good – but even with these good things, if you don't have the truth about salvation then you're in trouble. That's why love rejoices with the truth. If you truly love others you should want to share the gospel with them. You should be glad to hear of other people sharing the gospel and of people being saved from their sins.

Is your heart glad? Or maybe it's troubled?

Let's Read
Turn in your Bible to Mark 10:17-22

As Jesus started on his way, a man ran up to him and fell on his knees before him. 'Good teacher,' he asked, 'what must I do to inherit eternal life?' 'Why do you call me good?' Jesus answered. 'No one is good – except God alone. You know the commandments: "Do not murder, do not commit adultery, do not steal, do not give false testimony, do not defraud, honour your father and mother."' 'Teacher,' he declared, 'all these I have kept since I was a boy.' Jesus looked at him and loved him. 'One thing you lack,' He

104

said. 'Go, sell everything you have and give to the poor, and you will have treasure in heaven. Then come, follow me.' At this the man's face fell. He went away sad, because he had great wealth.

A young man wanted to know how to be saved. But Jesus knew this young man's heart. So He told the young man to keep the commandments – to which the young man replied, 'This I have done since I was a young boy.'

Wow – even though he had probably never murdered anyone or stolen anything, the young man also thought that he had never disobeyed his parents or worshipped idols. He was wrong. We have all disobeyed our parents, haven't we? And as for worshipping idols – well, we will soon see that the young man did have an idol in his life.

Jesus went on to tell the young man that he needed to give away all his wealth. Is that really how we become Christians? By giving away money? No! But Jesus knew that this young man had made an idol of money and he needed to turn from that and give his heart to God. How tragic that the young man chose to love his riches rather than loving Jesus. He went away sad indeed.

Digging Deeper

- Jesus loved the young man, but He knew that his heart would not rejoice in the truth. Jesus wanted the young man to see he was a sinner – but the young man refused to believe it. Do you know that you are a sinner?

- Jesus wanted the young man to love Him more than he loved anything else. What did the young man love the most? How do you know that? What do you love most? How do you know?

- The young man wanted eternal life. What is eternal life? How do we get it? Read Acts 16:31.

- If you know that you do not have eternal life, perhaps you would like to stop here and pray, asking the Lord to forgive your sins and to change your heart so that you love Him more than anything else.

- If you want to, perhaps you could write your prayer here.

- If you know you have eternal life your heart should be so glad!
- Think of someone you know who doesn't love the Lord Jesus. Pray that they will come to know and love Him just as you do. Perhaps God would have you tell them about Him.

107

Let's Pray

Dear Lord, thank you that through Jesus we can have eternal life. I pray for those who I know do not yet love you and ask that you would show them their need for you. I pray that you would help me to share You with others so that I might obey your commands.

In Jesus' name,

Amen

In God We Trust

GOD'S WORD: PSALM 40:4

There were once three young men who put their trust in the true God and it made their king so furious that he threw them into a raging fiery furnace. Can you imagine your President or Prime Minister ordering you to be thrown into a fire because you worshipped God? Sadly, in some countries Christians are being killed for their faith in the Lord. But this has always been the case – even before Jesus came to the earth.

Now, these three young men worked for the king and served him well. So what did they do that made him so furious?

Let's Read
Turn in your Bible to Daniel 3:4-6

Then the herald loudly proclaimed, 'This is what you are commanded to do, O peoples, nations and men of every language: As soon as you hear the sound of the horn, flute, zither, lyre, harp, pipes and all kinds of music, you must fall down and worship the image of gold that King Nebuchadnezzar has set up. Whoever does not fall down and worship will immediately be thrown into a blazing furnace.' Therefore, as soon as they heard the sound of the horn, flute, zither, lyre, harp and all kinds of music, all the peoples, nations and men of every language fell down and worshipped the image of gold that King Nebuchadnezzar had set up. At this time some astrologers came forward and denounced the Jews. They said to King Nebuchadnezzar, 'O king, live forever! You have issued a decree, O king, that everyone who hears the sound of the horn, flute, zither, lyre, harp, pipes and all kinds of music must fall down and worship the image of gold, and that whoever does not fall down and worship will be thrown into a blazing furnace. But there are some Jews whom you have set over the affairs of the province of Babylon – Shadrach, Meshach and Abednego – who pay no attention to you, O king. They neither serve your gods nor worship the image of gold you have set up.'

Now we see the problem. The three young men loved God and they could not and would not worship an idol. Do you know what an idol is? It's something that becomes more important to us than anything else. It doesn't have to be a statue; it can be our favourite computer game or our friends. It can be money or our family or even the way we want to look. If it's the most important thing in your life, then it has become an idol.

Back to the three young men. It seems the king was a man of his word and he soon had the young men tied up and thrown into the fire. Read verses 16-18 of chapter 3 to see what the young man had said to the king before they were thrown into the fire.

Shadrach, Meshach and Abednego replied to the king, 'O Nebuchadnezzar, we do not need to defend ourselves before you in this matter. If we are thrown into the blazing furnace, the God we serve is able to save us from it, and he will rescue us from your hand, O king. But even if he does not, we want you to know, O king, that we will not serve your gods or worship the image of gold you have set up.'

Why did they say that? Couldn't they have just pretended to worship the idol and thus save their lives? No.

These three young men knew the truth. They served the one true God and they knew the blessing that comes from putting their faith and trust in God. They were determined to continue serving Him, even if it meant they would lose their earthly lives.

Digging Deeper

- What does it mean to 'put your trust in God'?
- Putting your trust in God means that you believe He is the True God and you give your life to Him, to serve Him and love Him above all else. That's just what the three young men did. They trusted in the Lord and lived their lives to serve Him and Him alone. How do you think the young men felt when they knew they were going to be thrown into the fire?

Let's Read

Turn in your Bible to Psalm 56:3-4

When I am afraid, I will trust in you. In God, whose word I praise, in God I trust; I will not be afraid. What can mortal man do to me?

Digging Deeper

- This is what the young men believed. They knew that even if they lost their lives they would be in heaven to be forever with their God. What things make you scared to tell people about Jesus? Remind your heart to trust in God.

- It seems like the king still didn't put his trust in the true God. Sometimes even when people know the truth they choose to continue to love the idols in their lives. Pray that God will protect your heart from trusting in idols and that He will help you love Him more.

Let's Pray

Dear God, thank you for the example the three young men are for us. They put their trust in you and they obeyed you even when it seemed they might lose their lives. Thank you that you saved them and showed that you are the true God. I pray you will help me to put my trust in you. Protect my heart from making idols and keep my eyes on you alone.

In Jesus' name,

Amen

Love Always Protects

GOD'S WORD: 1 CORINTHIANS 13:4-7

Have you ever heard someone call out, 'I'm telling on you!'

In my house we have a name for someone who uses those words. Maybe you do too. We call that person a 'tattle-tale'. A tattle-tale is someone who can't wait to tattle on someone. They love to get others in trouble by 'dobbing them in'.

Do you tattle-tale? I used to. I would be the first to run down the hallway to find my parents and tell them what naughty thing one of my brothers had done now. Maybe they had said a bad word or touched something they shouldn't have. I was wrong to be a tattle-tale.

I love my brothers dearly and have always loved them, but there were times that I did not show them love in my actions. Some of those times I was a tattle-tale instead of their loving sister.

115

Let's Read
Turn in your Bible to 1 Peter 4:8-11

Above all, love each other deeply, because love covers over a multitude of sins. Offer hospitality to one another without grumbling. Each one should use whatever gift he has received to serve others, faithfully administering God's grace in its various forms. If anyone speaks, he should do it as one speaking the very words of God. If anyone serves, he should do it with the strength God provides, so that in all things God may be praised through Jesus Christ. To him be the glory and the power for ever and ever. Amen.

There are some interesting things that we can learn from what Peter is writing.

Peter is writing to Christians who are being persecuted – that means that they are being hurt, put in prison, tortured and even killed just because they love and follow Jesus. Can you imagine that? People who were perhaps once their friends now hate them because they are Christians.

Instead of Peter telling the Christians to hide or leave that place he gives them some instructions on how to live in a way that pleases Jesus.

116

Imagine this: your family is in trouble for being Christians. There is a possibility that you will all be imprisoned, hurt and maybe even killed. Some in your church have already suffered and have lost loved ones. In fact some are even coming to your house for safety and for food and shelter. It's dangerous. The authorities are beginning to notice all the people that come and go from your home. The next knock on the door might be soldiers, ready to take you all to prison, or worse.

Your home is cramped – there are people everywhere, crying, praying, hiding. Your parents are trying to make food for everyone; babies are screaming; children are missing their daddies – it's horrible. To top it off, you are sharing your room with two other girls and they are being very unkind to you – stealing your things, complaining about your small house and the limited food. You are frustrated, sad and angry. What are your options? You could turn in all these folks to the authorities and hope they will grant your family protection in return. Or you could tell your parents about these girls, but this may cause arguments among the parents and others. Or you could choose to love the girls – to remind yourself that they are scared, worried and homesick. You could love them and

117

let your love cover over their sin; that would be protecting them and giving them a chance to put things right. Now, there are times when it is right to tell on someone – times when someone could be hurt or when their behaviour is dangerous. But other times might be an opportunity to show love and let your love cover over the wrong. Protect them and give them a chance to put things right.

Let's Read
Turn in your Bible to Proverbs 11:13

A gossip betrays a confidence,
but a trustworthy man keeps a secret.

The ESV Bible says it like this:
Whoever goes about slandering reveals secrets,
but he who is trustworthy in spirit
keeps a thing covered.

Digging Deeper

- Gossip is talking about someone to others. Sometimes gossip is true but, even so, we should not be a part of it if it will hurt the person it's about. Can you think of an example of gossip?

118

- If someone tells you some gossip (even if it is about someone that you don't really like) how can you show love?

- If someone tries to share gossip with you, the best way to show love is to refuse to hear it. That means that you are protecting the person whom the gossip is about. What can you say to stop a person from sharing gossip with you?

- The next time a brother or sister or kid at school does wrong and you want to tattle on them, what should you do instead?

Let's Pray

*D*ear Jesus, sometimes it is hard to see others doing something I know is wrong and not tell anyone about it. Help me to know when it is right to tell and when it is right to hold my tongue. I want to be able to show love which always protects – please help me understand more what that means and how I can do that.

Forgive me for the times that I have not shown love which always protects – and help me to be an example to others.

In your name, Jesus,

Amen

A Hurting Heart

GOD'S WORD: PSALM 62:1-6

Sometimes people hurt us with their actions and sometimes they hurt us with their words. They say unkind things – gossip – about us to others. Can you think of a time when others have spoken unkindly about you, about something you said or did – or maybe they just made it up? As we learned in the previous chapter, that is called gossip and the Bible tells us that gossip is a sin. Even though we know gossip is wrong, sometimes we still initiate or listen to it – or it is said of us. And it hurts; sometimes it hurts us very badly.

Psalm 62 reminds us that God is our protector and our comforter. In times when we have been hurt by others, God is always there to comfort us.

Let's Read
Turn in your Bible to Matthew 27:27-31

Then the governor's soldiers took Jesus into the Praetorium and gathered the whole company of soldiers round Him. They stripped Him and put a scarlet robe on Him, and then twisted together a crown of thorns and set it on His head. They put a staff in His right hand and knelt in front of Him and mocked Him. 'Hail, king of the Jews!' they said. They spit on Him, and took the staff and struck Him on the head again and again. After they had mocked Him, they took off the robe and put His own clothes on Him. Then they led Him away to crucify Him.

This is part of the account of the crucifixion of Jesus. At this point Jesus has been betrayed by Judas, one of His own disciples and friends.

Judas travelled with Jesus and the other disciples for three years. Jesus taught them all about God and how to reach the lost and care for the saved. At the end of that time together, Judas' life remained unchanged. He still loved himself more than anyone else, and he loved money more than anything.

Judas had been in charge of the disciples' money, looking after it and

122

using it to get what they needed, but he was also stealing it. He was taking some of it and putting it in his own wallet (John 12:6). And now Judas had betrayed Jesus for a few pieces of silver.

So here, the soldiers have come for Jesus according to Judas' instructions and now they are mocking Him and beating Him; spitting on Him and stripping Him of His clothes. How do you think this would make Jesus feel? I think I would have felt hurt – both physically because of the beating, but my heart would have hurt knowing that a friend had betrayed me. I would have felt humiliated, weak, distressed and lonely. I think that is what Jesus might have felt too. Then they crucified Him.

Jesus was the subject of torture, mockery, gossip and finally murder. How did He respond to all of that?

Let's Read
Turn in your Bible to Luke 23:32-34

Two other men, both criminals, were also led out with Him to be executed. When they came to the place called the Skull, there they crucified Him, along with the criminals – one on His right, the other on His left. Jesus said, 'Father, forgive them, for they do

123

not know what they are doing.' And they divided up His clothes by casting lots.

Jesus forgave them, just as He forgives you and me when we sin. Jesus is our example, and that is one of the ways in which He comforts us. He provides us with the example and the strength to follow His example. Is your heart hurting at the moment because of someone who has sinned against you? Follow the example of Jesus and forgive them. Forgive and pray.

Digging Deeper

- Did Jesus ask God to take revenge on those who had hurt Him? What did He ask God to do?
- Why did Jesus ask God to forgive the people instead of asking God to hurt them?
- Jesus shows us the greatest example of love. Even though many people hated Jesus, Jesus loved them deeply. Can you think of someone who you need to forgive and love? Or perhaps you have hurt someone and you need to ask for their forgiveness.

124

Let's Pray

ear Lord, it makes me sad to think that people were so unkind to You even though You came to forgive and save them from their sin. I know I am a sinner and I thank you that you chose to forgive and die on that cross even though not one of us deserves that forgiveness. Thank you for your example to me in times of trial – please help me to be like you when others are being unkind to me. Help me to be someone who forgives and covers over sin.

In your name, Jesus,

Amen

Love Always Trusts

GOD'S WORD: 1 CORINTHIANS 13:4-7

Another way to say 'trust' is to say 'believe the best'. Instead of saying, 'I trust you,' you can say, 'I will believe the best about you'. What does that mean? It means that you choose to believe the best of those you love. Instead of jumping to conclusions and thinking that your friends are laughing at you when you walk out of the room, you can choose to believe the best – that they were just telling a funny joke. Or instead of getting mad at your sister because she broke your favourite necklace, you can choose instead to believe it was an accident and comfort her so she doesn't feel bad.

There is an example in the Bible of friends who did not believe the best of another friend. It caused terrible hurt to this friend and God had to chastise them for their foolishness. I wonder if you can guess who I am talking about?

Let's Read
Turn in your Bible to Job 4:5-8

But now trouble comes to you, and you are discouraged; it strikes you, and you are dismayed. Should not your piety be your confidence and your blameless ways your hope? 'Consider now: Who, being innocent, has ever perished? Where were the upright ever destroyed? As I have observed, those who plow evil and those who sow trouble reap it.'

Job was a righteous and blameless man. He loved the Lord and lived a life of obedience to God. However, Satan believed that Job was only obedient because his life was easy. Job was a wealthy man and he had many sons and daughters, servants and animals. Satan believed that if Job lost all of these then he would turn away from God. That would mean that Job only loved God if God did what Job wanted him to do. Sometimes we are all tempted to think that way, but no – not Job. God told Satan to go ahead and cause a time of trial for Job – the loss of all he had except the lives of him and his wife. And that is what happened.

When terrible and sad things happen to us or our loved ones, we

128

need and want the comfort of friends and family; those who can listen and love us and give us wise advice. Instead, what Job got was more grief and trouble from his friends.

The verses above from Job 4 record just a very small part of what one of his supposed friends said to him as he was grieving over all that had happened. Can you understand what the friend was saying?

The friend was saying that all the bad things had happened because Job was being punished for something he had done. Was this true? No! Was this helpful or hurtful to Job? It was hurtful!

Let's Read
Turn in your Bible to Job 1:1-3

In the land of Uz there lived a man whose name was Job. This man was blameless and upright; he feared God and shunned evil. He had seven sons and three daughters, and he owned seven thousand sheep, three thousand camels, five hundred yoke of oxen and five hundred donkeys, and had a large number of servants. He was the greatest man among all the people of the East.

Job's friend was speaking foolishness. God in fact called Job a man who feared God and shunned evil. That is exactly the opposite of what his

129

friend was saying. But it gets worse. More friends come along and they bombard poor Job with more of the same – saying he must have done something to deserve punishment from God.

If Job's friends had believed the best of Job then they could have come alongside their friend and comforted him and encouraged him.

If you read through Job you will see that eventually God rebukes the friends and He blesses Job and restores all that was taken from him and more. But what a shame that Job did not have his friends to bear the burden with him. What a shame that sometimes we also respond in the same way.

Digging Deeper

- Can you think of a time when you chose not to think the best of friends or family? What happened? What should you have done instead? How have you made that situation right?
- Sometimes it is hard to think the best – but we can do all things through Jesus who gives us strength. Why would Jesus help us to think the best of people?

- If showing love is to think the best, what does it show when we do not think the best?

Let's Pray

Dear Lord, thank you that we can learn from Job and the hard time he went through. Please help us to fear you and shun evil just as Job did. And please help us to choose to think the best in all situations as you give us strength and wisdom.

In Jesus' name,

Amen

Believe the Best

GOD'S WORD: PSALM 91:14-16

God wants what is best for us. In fact He also promises that for those who love Him, whatever happens He will make them more like Him because that is what is best for them. Do you know where that promise is in your Bible?

Let's Read
Turn in your Bible to Romans 8:28

And we know that in all things God works for the good of those who love him, who have been called according to his purpose.

Sometimes there are things in life which can cause us great hurt and sadness. The verse in Romans promises that in these times God works for our good. Sometimes what we think is good is not what God thinks is best for us – and sometimes that can be hard for us to understand. But we must remember one thing: God loves all the time, every day, without ever changing or ceasing. We must believe the best about God – and the best is that He is love.

Let's Read
Turn in your Bible to James 1:2-4

Consider it pure joy, my brothers, whenever you face trials of many kinds, because you know that the testing of your faith develops perseverance. Perseverance must finish its work so that you may be mature and complete, not lacking anything.

James tells us that when Christians go through a trial they can be happy – not happy to be in tough times, or happy about whatever is happening, but happy that God will use it to make them more like Him.

There are times when terrible things happen. When there was a huge earthquake and tsunami in Japan many people died: mothers and fathers, children, brothers, sisters, aunts and uncles, friends. It's a tragedy that I hope will never happen to you. But no doubt we will face something sad during our lives and we must remember at those times that God is good and He loves us. That might seem obvious right now — but when our hearts are hurting and the tears are streaming down our faces, we need to remember that truth. Sometimes we might be tempted to think that God doesn't care. But He does. John 3:16 reminds us just how much God loves us.

When we go through a tough time we can allow God to use that time to make us more like Him. How?

First, we must trust Him. We must believe the best about God. We must believe that God loves us and that He knows why these things happen, even if we don't.

Then we must pray to God for help and strength. We do our best, with God's help, to be obedient even when our hearts are hurting. The Apostle Paul has some advice ... Look back at Romans 8:28.

What does it mean to be more like the Lord? It means we will love others more, care for others better, know more of God and walk more closely with Him each day so that we can give Him glory by the way that we live.

For the people in Japan, their lives were changed forever. Those who survived suffered terribly because of all they went through. But those who

135

love Jesus, even in their sadness, will be drawn closer to Him. They will grow more like Him and be better equipped to serve and love others because of their suffering. And it all starts with believing the best about God.

Digging Deeper

- Is there a time when you have felt let down by or angry with God? What made you feel that way?
- What is true about God in any situation? What is true about the way God thinks about you in any situation?
- Sometimes we don't understand why God allows sad things to happen. What should we remind ourselves about God when we are sad?
- How can you encourage or comfort someone to trust in God when they are going through a hard time?

Let's Pray

Dear God, even though terrible things happen, you are always a God of love and want the best for me. Sometimes what I think is best may not be what you know is best. Help me during those times to trust in you. You are all-wise. Help me to encourage others to trust in you too.

In Jesus' name,

Amen.

Love Always Hopes

GOD'S WORD: 1 CORINTHIANS 13:4-7

In 1793 a young man named William Carey sailed on a ship from England. He took with him his wife, Dorothy, their four young children and his sister-in-law. It would have been a terrible journey in cramped conditions with storms, sea sickness and not even a proper bathroom to use. Yuck! It doesn't sound like a great family holiday, does it?

Well, that is because it wasn't. William was taking his family to India because he loved the Lord with all his heart and he felt desperate that the Indian people should hear the gospel of the Lord Jesus so that they too could be saved.

Can you imagine what it would have been like in India back in the 1700s? No fancy hotels to stay in with restaurants and swimming pools, no internet or email or even telephone to contact family back home. There would have been diseases, dangerous animals, and people who looked different. There would have been lots of languages and unknown foods. How brave this little family must have been, and how strong their desire for the gospel to be preached in India!

It would be great if I could tell you that not long after William started to share the gospel in India many people came to know and love Jesus as their Lord, but that isn't what happened. In fact it was seven long years before one person got saved. Seven years!

That's a long time to keep telling people about Jesus and not seeing anyone respond. William kept at it though because he had hope in the Lord. His hope was that people would be saved. William knew that it was not him who could save – only the Lord by His mighty power would save people from their sins. However, William determined in his heart to be faithful and continue to tell the gospel hoping for even one convert.

Well, there was a convert, several. In fact William Carey is now known as the father of modern missions and through his example and influence many people all over the world have been saved by the gospel.

William, however, spent many hours on his knees praying for these precious souls, loving them, serving

140

them, studying their language so he could share the Bible in their language. William hoped – and God was faithful and rewarded William's hope. Imagine the celebrations the day that first man came to know Jesus Christ as his Lord and Saviour!

Let's Read

Turn in your Bible to Matthew 28:19-20

Therefore go and make disciples of all nations, baptizing them in the name of the Father and of the Son and of the Holy Spirit, and teaching them to obey everything I have commanded you. And surely I am with you always, to the very end of the age.

Jesus was telling His disciples to go and make more disciples. What does that mean? It means that they (and we, if we trust in the Lord Jesus) are to go and tell others the good news of Jesus Christ, the one who came to offer forgiveness of sins and eternal life to sinners.

That is exactly what William did. He went to India. We don't have to go to India though – we can go to our brother or sister, friend or cousin, teacher or neighbour. It just means that we should go and find those who don't love the Lord and tell them about Him so they too

141

can be saved. Notice, the verses don't talk about how many people will be saved or how soon it will happen after we tell them the gospel – or even if they will get saved. Only God knows those things. We don't need to know. We just need to go. Go, and hope that people will become Christians because if they don't, they won't go to heaven. That is how we love others. Tell them the gospel so that they can be saved – then we keep on hoping and keep on praying for them.

Digging Deeper

- Who do you know who isn't a Christian, whom you can pray for and share the gospel with?
- How long should you pray for someone to become a Christian? Should we ever stop praying for someone to be saved?
- What would you say to a friend who asked you how they could become a Christian? Practise telling this to a parent, Sunday School teacher or pastor – so they can help you to be ready to share the gospel. Write it out so that you can remember what the important things to say are.

Let's Pray

*D*ear God, thank you for the example of William Carey who went to India to tell people about you. Thank you that he was patient even though it was a long time before anyone was saved. Thank you that you have saved many people in India and I pray that you will continue to use missionaries there and around the world to teach the good news about your Son, Jesus Christ. Please help me to be a missionary in whatever place you have me.

In Jesus' name,

Amen

I Hope

GOD'S WORD: PSALM 130:5

Did you know that there are different meanings of the word 'hope'? Can you think of two sentences using these different meanings?

Let me show you.

1. 'I hope we will have ice-cream after dinner.'
2. 'My hope is in the Lord.'

The first sentence is about something that we want, but it is uncertain whether or not we will get it. There might not be any in the freezer!

The second sentence expresses a certainty. We could say 'trust' instead of 'hope' in this sentence: 'My trust is in the Lord'. The writer of the Psalm put his hope (or trust) in the Word of God. He believed that what is written in the Bible is inspired and from the mouth of God and is all totally true (2 Timothy 3:16-17). That means that if the Bible promises eternal life to those who believe in Jesus and repent of their sins, that is exactly what the person will receive – eternal life.

Here's another example of hoping or trusting in the Lord. When you sit in a chair, you know or trust that the chair will hold you. You put all of your weight into that chair because you want to rest in it – you want your body to rest and regain energy. It's the same when we trust in God. We trust Him completely knowing that He won't let us down. He keeps His promises, His Word is true, He loves us without us having to earn His love – we can rest in all of that.

I wonder if you have put your trust in God? It simply means that you have become a Christian – that you live for Him and trust that He will help you in every area of your life. He will help you in your love for Him, in your obedience, your attitudes towards others, your understanding of His Word and knowing how to live out what He asks of you.

He will also help you with your desires, talents, hopes and dreams. Ask God that he will use all these things, your whole life, for His wonderful plan.

Have you done this?

146

Let's Read
Turn in your Bible to Isaiah 40:30-31

*E*ven youths grow tired and weary, and young men stumble and fall; but those who hope in the LORD will renew their strength. They will soar on wings like eagles; they will run and not grow weary, they will walk and not be faint.

When we go through life without putting our hope in the Lord, a few things will happen. We will get tired. We will put a great deal of energy into the life that we think best – life without God's wisdom, life without God's peace and comfort; that is tiring.

We will probably also feel discouraged because we will feel that we are not good enough or not successful enough.

We will also become selfish because it's hard enough to live for oneself without having to care for others as well! That's not a great sounding life, is it?

God's Word promises that when we hope in Him we will have our strength renewed – strength to live for Him and strength for serving others. Will we really fly on wings like eagles or run without

147

getting tired? No – the verse simply means that when our hope is in the Lord, He will enable us to do things that we couldn't do in our own strength.

And finally, we can hope for others – hope that others who we love will also be shown God's grace and mercy just as we have been; that they too will come to know and love Jesus as Saviour. Is there someone you have been praying for to become a Christian? God's Word tells you that love always hopes – hopes for their salvation by praying faithfully for them and loving them selflessly.

Digging Deeper

- How do we know if our hope is in the Lord?
- If our hope is in the Lord do we honour God?
- Do we choose to do it every day in prayer and in doing all that we do to honour God?
- To put your hope in the Lord means you have to be a Christian. Are you a Christian?
- Is there someone who you hope will become a Christian? Have you prayed today that they will be saved? If not, do that now.
- Write a poem or prayer thanking God for the hope you have in Him.

Let's Pray

Dear Lord, thank you for the hope that we can have in you. This hope is not only for us, but also for those we love who do not know you, so please help us to pray faithfully for them. Thank you that we can trust you always.

In Jesus' name,

Amen

29

Love Always Perseveres

GOD'S WORD: 1 CORINTHIANS 13:4-7

There is a movie that my family like to watch. It's about a little fish who lives in the big ocean with his dad. One day this little fish chooses to disobey his father and as a result is taken from the ocean to live in a fish tank miles away from home. The father is determined to do whatever he needs to do in order to rescue his son, but encounters many difficulties – fish eating sharks, stinging jellyfish, getting lost, being swallowed by a whale and many, many miles to swim.

Along the journey the father makes a friend and just when poor old dad fish is so discouraged and ready to give up, the friend encourages him to 'keep on swimming!' In other words 'don't give up! Keep going!'

That is what perseverance means, it means keep trying even when it's very hard to, and don't give up.

Let's Read
Turn in your Bible to Galatians 6:9-10

Let us not become weary in doing good, for at the proper time we will reap a harvest if we do not give up. Therefore, as we have opportunity, let us do good to all people, especially to those who belong to the family of believers.

Sometimes it's hard for us to love one another, especially if the person is unkind or just annoying! We would probably prefer to ignore them and not to even go near them. But that's not right.

The Bible tells us that we are to love our neighbour as we love ourselves and we already know that our neighbour is anyone! They might be next door, or it might be a kid at school or the lady in line next to us in the grocery store. Or maybe it's the folks that we are reading about in the paper who have suffered a terrible tragedy.

We are called to love all people. Love is not just a feeling – it's also our actions and attitudes. So we can show people love by helping them and being kind to them. In fact, it really seems by now that real love is more about doing and attitudes than about our feelings, don't you think?

152

Some of the ways you can show love to your neighbour might be something like helping them with some homework that they find hard. Or showing them something new you have learnt on your guitar or computer game, or even just including them when you do things with your other friends.

However, if that person is unkind or if they embarrass us because they seem different to us and our friends, we can be tempted to walk away from them. Would that be showing love?

Sometimes there is a need to walk away from a situation, but we should be slow to do that. There is usually a reason why someone is unkind or mean – and maybe we can help them. Maybe they are jealous of you, or perhaps they are having a really hard time at home.

The Apostle Paul wrote to the Galatians saying, 'Let us not become weary in doing good' (Galatians 6:9). I want to encourage you to do the same. Don't become tired of showing love – especially when it's hard and not returned to you. Keep on trying with that person. There may be a time, because of the love you have shown, that person will look to Jesus for help. You kept on loving them even when they were hard to love. Does that remind you of anyone,

153

I wonder? It reminds me of me. I know that sometimes I am hard to love, but Jesus keeps on loving me, and He always will. That is what He has promised. God has said, 'Never will I leave you; never will I forsake you' (Hebrews 13:5). That means that God will never turn His back on those who love Him even when we are horrible and selfish! Jesus is our example. Jesus perseveres in love with us – He keeps on loving. That's what we should be like. Remember to keep on persevering.

Digging Deeper

- Is there someone you find it hard to show love to? What is it that makes it so hard for you to love them?
- How do you normally respond to them?
- What would be the loving way to respond to them?
- Maybe you already do show them love and that is wonderful! But if not, don't be discouraged, tomorrow is a new day, a day in which you can choose to be someone who perseveres in love.
  - What could you do to show that person your love for them?

154

- How can you pray for your own heart, asking the Lord to help you show love? Do you need help to show patience, or selflessness or courage? Perhaps you need help to speak kind words or to speak up for someone. Perhaps you need to ask forgiveness for the way in which you have not shown love.
- Write that prayer and put it somewhere you can see it each day so you can keep on praying about that need.

Let's Pray

Dear Father God, I am so thankful that you choose to love me and to keep on loving me. I know that there are times when I am hard to love, just as there are times that those around me are hard for me to love. Please forgive me for the times when I have not shown love to someone and instead have caused them hurt. Help me to make things right if I need to. And please help me to love those who annoy me or have been unkind to me, so that I can show them your love.

In Jesus' name,
Amen.

30

Are You Blessed?

GOD'S WORD: PSALM 1

Did you know that the Bible is the true Word of God? That means that whatever the Bible says is not only absolutely true, but if it's telling us to do something then we absolutely must do it! Why? Because God loves us so much that He has given us His Word, the Bible, as a guide and whatever He has written for us in this book is the best for us.

Sometimes our parents seem to be asking us to do things that do not seem the best for us or the most fun. But I can promise you that for the most part, parents have your best interests at heart and they are trying their absolute best to protect you, love you and provide for you. Now, as a parent I am the first to admit that sometimes I get it wrong. Sometimes my decisions are not always the best – but the decisions I make are because I love my children and want the best for them. That is the same with God – except that God never gets it wrong. Whatever He has for us to do – or not to do – is really the right thing. Even if at the time it doesn't feel to us like it is.

As we have looked together at 1 Corinthians 13:4-7 about love, we have learnt a lot together. We have learnt that love is not just a feeling – there is a lot of 'doing' that is involved when you love someone. And sometimes it's hard to love! But God gives us guidelines in the Bible as to how best to love people. Something else that we have learnt is that this true love which the Bible teaches us can only be shown by those who love the Lord Jesus, those who we call Christians. I know that there are people who are not Christians who are very kind and loving – but I am talking about this love that we learn of in the Bible. We can try all we like to love others this way, but if we do not love Jesus with all our hearts, then the truth is that we will always love ourselves more than we love others.

Let's Read
Turn in your Bible to Psalm 1:1-3

Blessed is the man who does not walk in the counsel of the wicked or stand in the way of sinners or sit in the seat of mockers.

But his delight is in the law of the LORD, and on his law he meditates day and night. He is like a tree planted by streams of water, which yields its fruit in season and whose leaf does not wither.

Psalm 1 reminds us of the blessing that it is to love the Lord Jesus and His Word. Why don't you read through Psalm 1 again and then we can look together at a few things in a little more detail.

Digging Deeper

- What does 'blessed' mean?
- 'Blessed' means happy. Instead of saying 'blessed is the man (or girl) who does not walk in the counsel of sinners' you could say, 'happy is the man (or girl) who does not walk in the counsel (or in the example or advice) of sinners'.
- Why do you think that someone who does not walk in the ways of sinners would be happy?
- To have our sins taken away from us is a wonderful and most precious gift. To know we will one day spend eternity with Jesus and with all those who love Jesus, is also an exciting thought! But there is even more.

159

Psalm 1 tells us that a Christian who loves God will prosper. That means that he or she will grow to be more like Jesus. Why is that so wonderful?

- Psalm 1 tells us that Christians, who love and obey God, will show fruit in their lives. We have already looked at what it means to bear fruit in our lives (if you can't remember turn back to Chapter 14 for a reminder). The more fruitful we are, the more we will love as God wants us to love.

- Are you a Christian? If so, do you or others around you (your parents, your best friends) see fruit in your life? In what areas do you think you need to improve?

Let's Pray

Dear Lord, it has been so good to learn about love – your kind of love.

We know that if we are Christians, we have no option other than to show others this kind of love

love that is patient, kind,

love that does not envy or boast,

love that is not rude or easily angered,

160

love that keeps no record of wrongs,
love that does not delight in evil but rejoices
with truth,
love that always protects, always trusts, always
hopes and always perseveres.

This is a hard kind of love to have – but I want
to show it because it is what is best and it is how
you want me to be. Lord, please work in my own
heart so that I might love you with all my heart,
soul and mind and that I might love others as I
love myself. Thank you Lord for loving me.

In Jesus' name,
Amen

How do I Become a Christian?

UNDERSTAND THAT GOD IS HOLY

1 Samuel 2:2a says, 'There is no one holy like the LORD.'

When we say that God is holy, we mean that He is without sin. God is pure and separate from anything evil. God created us to enjoy a friendship with Him where we grow to know Him, and respond to Him by loving, worshipping and obeying Him as the centre of our lives.

UNDERSTAND THAT YOU ARE A SINNER

Romans 3:10 says, 'There is no one righteous, not even one.'

Romans 3:23 says, 'for all have sinned and fall short of the glory of God.'

Sadly, we are unable to enjoy this friendship with God because of sin. Sin is anything that displeases God or fails to meet His standards. In order for us to be right with God, we need to be righteous people. Righteous means perfect in the eyes of God, but the Bible says that no one is like this; everyone has sinned. Sin not only separates us from God, but also makes us God's enemies rather than His friends. Unless we can have our sins forgiven, we will never know God and receive eternal life. We are, instead, in danger of receiving God's punishment for our sins and because God's standard is perfection, there is nothing that we can do on our own to change our bad situation.

UNDERSTAND THAT FORGIVENESS REQUIRES A SACRIFICE

Hebrews 9:22b says, 'Without the shedding of blood there is no forgiveness.'

In order to receive God's forgiveness in the old days, God required people to bring a perfect lamb or goat to the priests at the temple. The animal would be sacrificed (which showed that the animal was being punished instead of the person) and the sinner would then be forgiven by God. God also promised that one day He would provide a greater sacrifice which would take away sin once and for all. This sacrifice would not be an animal; God would give His one and only Son, Jesus Christ.

UNDERSTAND THAT JESUS CAME TO PAY THE PRICE FOR OUR SIN

John 1:29 says, 'Look, the Lamb of God, who takes away the sin of the world!'

God sent Jesus, His only precious and perfect Son, to die in our place and take the punishment that we deserve. He was born as a baby in Bethlehem, grew up in a family in the land of Israel, and at the age of about 30 began a special mission in order to obey His Father's plan to rescue sinners. This meant that He would later be mistreated and suffer a cruel death by being nailed to a cross of wood, even though He had done nothing wrong. But God raised Jesus from the dead on the third day and, now, because of Jesus' sacrifice, God offers everyone forgiveness and the invitation to know Him.

UNDERSTAND THAT WE MUST RECEIVE GOD'S OFFER OF FORGIVENESS

John 3:16 says, 'For God so loved the world that he gave his one and only Son, that whoever believes in him shall not perish but have eternal life.'

In order to receive God's gift of forgiveness and come into a right relationship with Him, we must:

165

ADMIT that we have sinned against God and be willing to turn away from our sins (repent).

BELIEVE that Jesus is the Son of God (He is God in human form) and that He paid the penalty for our sins when he died on the cross, and that He rose again from the dead.

FOLLOW the Lord Jesus in your life. He gives you the strength to live for Him each day.

When I was your age, adults would talk about 'the sinners prayer'. It is a prayer that was prayed from the heart, telling Jesus that you believe He is the Son of God who came to earth to be the sacrifice for the sin of the world; to ask for His forgiveness; and to commit your life to following God for all your days. It is the prayer of a sinner asking God to save them from their sin.

Let's Pray

Dear God, I believe that you sent your Son Jesus to earth to die on the cross and take the punishment for the sin of the world. I believe He rose again and that He is now in heaven with You. I know that I am a sinner and I ask for your forgiveness. And I ask you to help me to follow you for all my days. Thank you for loving me.

In Jesus' name,

Amen.

Personal Pages

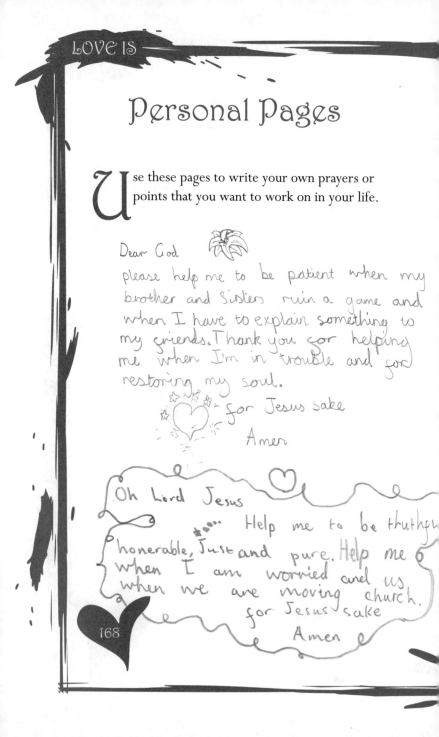

Use these pages to write your own prayers or points that you want to work on in your life.

Dear God

please help me to be patient when my brother and sisters ruin a game and when I have to explain something to my friends. Thank you for helping me when I'm in trouble and for restoring my soul.

- for Jesus sake

Amen

Oh Lord Jesus

Help me to be thuthful honerable, Just and pure. Help me when I am worried and us when we are moving church.

for Jesus sake

Amen

168

Our Father in heaven

Hallowed be your name,

Your kingdom come,
your will be done,

On earth as it is in heaven,

Give us this day our daily bread,

and Forgive us our debts,

as we also have forgiven our
debtors,

And lead us not into temptation

but but deliver us from

Evil.

Oh Lord
    Help me to make you my most
important thing not money or earthly thing
Help me to trust you and to have faith
in you,

Thank you that I am well and healthy,

Lord please help me to be kind to people
who are trying to help even if it isn't,

Please forgive my sins,

Thank you for welcoming sinners like
me and

Thank you coming to our world to
save my sins.
                    Amen

• Be more patient
• Dont be jealous

170

A Note From the Author

My name is Laura Martin and I'm married to Bryan. We have four beautiful children and a crazy spaniel. I serve alongside my husband who is pastor of River City Bible Church – a church we planted in Hamilton, New Zealand in 2010. Prior to that we were serving in a church in the U.K. I home-school our children, enjoy travelling, gardening, quilting, projects around the house, and writing. I love to disciple and counsel young women from God's precious Word.

I wrote 'Love Is' because I wanted to teach my children what it means to love one another biblically. The project also reminded me of how wonderful and sacrificial the love of God is towards us.

The aim of 'Love Is', is to show the person and character of God through His precious Word, which will cause our hearts to love Him and love one another truly!

Thank you for reading!

Laura Martin

Laura Martin's book, *Love Is … A Book for Girls About Love*, is a delightfully engaging devotional for young girls. Our daughter is now grown, but I remember searching for a book just like this one—and not finding it. How I wish this book had been available then! Laura Martin's love for children comes through on every page. It's like inviting her into your living room and having her lovingly teach your daughter a Bible study lesson.

Each devotion focuses on an aspect of love and how it's seen in God's character. Every chapter contains a short Bible story or true-to-life anecdote and specific Scripture passages, followed by some Bible study questions, and a closing prayer of reflection for each girl to pray. I have to admit the Bible study questions in the 'Digging Deeper' section were my favorite part of the book. Laura Martin does what few people are able to do. She writes Bible study questions for children that are clear, direct, tied to the scriptures, and mentally engaging. I would recommend this little treasure based on that alone, but there's so much more here.

Lisa Hughes
Author of *God's Priorities for Today's Woman: Discovering His Plan for You*

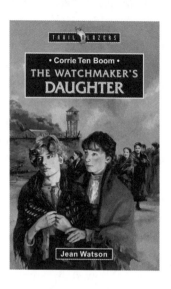

Corrie ten Boom: The Watchmaker's Daughter
by Jean Watson
ISBN: 978-1-85792-116-8

The story of Corrie ten Boom has inspired millions of people all over the world. Jean Watson is a skilful author and presents Corrie's stirring life and challenging hope-filled message for young readers.

The Watchmaker's Daughter traces the life of this outstanding Christian woman from her childhood in Haarlem, through her suffering in Nazi concentration camps, to her world-wide ministry to the handicapped and underprivileged.

This exciting victorious book will allow you to meet this beloved woman and learn of God's wonderful provision and blessing through adversity.

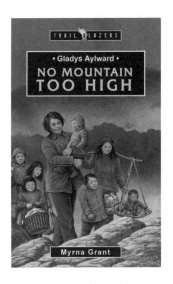

Gladys Aylward: No Mountain Too High
by Myrna Grant
ISBN: 978-1-85792-594-4

Many looked on Gladys Aylward's expedition to mainland China as foolhardy and dangerous. It was.

After having purchased her one-way ticket to China she left the United Kingdom with a single-minded determination to do what God had commanded her to. She knew she was meant to go to China – even if no mission was prepared to support her.

Unconventional is the only way to describe this journey to the country that would eventually become her home. A theme that would continue throughout her mission work in China, where she thwarted authorities, became involved in the Chinese resistance and rescued over 100 children from the invading Japanese army.

CHRISTIAN FOCUS PUBLICATIONS

Christian Focus   Christian Heritage   CF4K   Mentor

Christian Focus Publications publishes books for adults and children under its four main imprints: Christian Focus, CF4K, Mentor and Christian Heritage. Our books reflect our conviction that God's Word is reliable and Jesus is the way to know him, and live for ever with him.

Our children's publication list includes a Sunday school curriculum that covers pre-school to early teens, and puzzle and activity books. We also publish personal and family devotional titles, biographies and inspirational stories that children will love.

If you are looking for quality Bible teaching for children then we have an excellent range of Bible stories and age-specific theological books.

From pre-school board books to teenage apologetics, we have it covered!

**Find us at our web page:
www.christianfocus.com**

CF4 •K
Because you're never
too young to know Jesus